Once upon a time...

Parenting
through
Storytelling

By Hoda Beshir

With a special Foreword by
Dr. Ekram and Dr. M. Rida Beshir

amana publications

amana publications
10710 Tucker Street
Beltsville, MD 20705-2223 USA
Tel: (301) 595-5999
Fax: (301) 595-5888

Email: amana@igprinting.com
Website: amana-publications.com

Library of Congress Cataloging-in-Publication Data

Beshir, Hoda.
  Once upon a time– : parenting through storytelling / by Hoda Beshir ;
with a special foreword by Dr. Ekram and Dr. M. Rida Beshir.– 1st ed.
    p. cm.
  Includes bibliographical references.
  ISBN 1-59008-038-6
  1. Child rearing–Religious aspects–Islam. 2. Parenting–Religious
aspects–Islam. 3. Muslim children–Conduct of life. 4. Islamic
stories. I. Title.

  HQ769.3.B477 2005
  297.5'77–dc22

                                              2005024189

Printed in the United States of America by International Graphics
10710 Tucker Street, Beltsville, Maryland 20705-2223 USA
Tel: (301) 595-5999 Fax: (301) 595-5888
Website: igprinting.com
E-mail: ig@igprinting.com

Acknowledgments

First and foremost, I would like to thank Allah *swt* for affording me this opportunity and for His countless blessings and bounties.

I would like to thank my Mom & Dad for the stories they told me growing up, for the wisdom with which they corrected me, for the sharing and telling and listening and bonding that was so important in my childhood and that still touches me so deeply today. Thank you for your gentle nudges in taking on this project. Thank you for your endless contributions, for the hours upon hours, for your energy and devotion in taking this book from an idea to a reality. As usual, your advice & persuasiveness led me to a marvelous new experience that I wouldn't have dreamt of on my own.

I would like to thank my sister Sumaiya for her endless reviewing and editing of this book. Thank you for your midnight reviews, the jokes, the emails, and the (many a secret) chuckles! Thanks for keeping it light.

I would like to thank my sister Noha for her gracious accommodations of my crunch time during this very special and busy time in her life. Thanks for being my lifelong writing buddy, for the poetry & the writing marathons & the sharing.

Wa Khitaamuhu Misk
I would like to thank my husband Mohamed for his endless patience & support through the writing of this book. Thanks for the "Once upon a time. . . ", for the encouragement, for the *dua*, for the silent nudges and smiles. I felt them all.

May Allah *swt* bless you all and accept your intentions and your actions for His sake alone.

Dedication

For my beloved niece and nephew,
Yasmeen & Mostafa
and their loving, patient parents,
Amirah & Mohamed
Hoping you will find it fun & useful.

For my supportive husband
and father-to-be, Mohamed,
And our expected baby,
In anticipation of sitting all together,
In the comfort of a story,
And sharing & telling & listening & bonding
& growing together,
Insha'a Allah.

Table of Contents

Foreword

ssalaamu alaikum wa rahmatullahi wa barakaatuh. In the name of Allah, most Gracious, most Merciful.

This book, which we have been thinking about for many years, has by Allah's grace finally become a reality.

The need for this book became apparent to us over the past several years. In our first book, *Meeting the Challenge of Parenting in the West: An Islamic Perspective,* we advised parents to use storytelling as a method for *tarbiyah,* as Allah models this for us in the *Qur'an* and the Prophet *saaw* models it for us in the *Seerah.* We discussed the effectiveness of this technique, having used it ourselves and seen how well it works.

Throughout the following years, while we were traveling to different communities to deliver our parenting workshops, we often received questions from concerned parents about different problem behaviors that their young children were doing again and again. They wanted to know how to deal with the behavior. Oftentimes, our answer was "use stories as one of the methods to deal with the problem." Many parents replied that they could not tell their children stories about their misbehaviour because they couldn't invent stories.

And so, for years we have been hoping to write a collection of stories for common misbehaviors. Earlier this year, we proposed the idea to our daughter Hoda and urged her to take on the project. We held several dis-cussions and collaborated with her on the ideas in this book, letting her take the literary lead.

We are very happy with the final product and enjoyed listening to story after story as Hoda told them to us. The stories in this book are an invaluable tool for any parent to use to correct specific behaviors and instill important Islamic concepts and beliefs in their children. They are also interesting and amusing, easily keeping the listener's attention.

Another great benefit to be taken from the stories in this book is the modeled behavior for parents. Many of the parenting concepts and techniques that are presented to parents sometimes remain abstract or theoretical. Through these stories, we have the rare ability to demonstrate the parenting strategies in detail. The stories provide you with the unique experience of "watching" as other parents model the recommended parenting behaviors. The modeling is expanded on in the section after each story, where the modeled behavior is pointed out explicitly so parents can look to it and apply it with their own children.

We would like to take this opportunity to thank our daughter Hoda for stepping up to the plate and taking on this important project to fill a huge gap in our Islamic library. We also want to congratulate her for doing such a wonderful job. For sure, it will be a great joy for us to use these stories with our own grandchildren.

We are hopeful that *insha'a* Allah, this book will be of great benefit to you and that you and your children will enjoy the stories as much as we did and learn from them in as many ways as possible. May Allah *swt* bless your efforts and ease your struggles.

Wasalaamu alaikum wa rahmatullahi wa barakaatuh.

– Dr. Ekram Beshir & Dr. Mohamed Rida Beshir

Chapter 1:
Introduction - Storytelling,
A Tool for Raising Children

Storytelling in the *Qur'an* and *Seerah*

Storytelling is a very effective method of *tarbiyah*. The *Qur'an* includes many stories that are used as means and ways of *tarbiyah* for Muslims. These stories can be divided into three categories.[1] The first category is that of the Stories of the Prophets. In them, Allah describes different incidents and events that prophets have experienced throughout their lives. Examples of such stories include the stories of Prophet Ibrahim, Prophet Musa, Prophet Isa, and Prophet Yusuf *aa*. The second category is that of historical stories that present specific individuals living in certain situations. Though the *Qur'an* identifies who the individuals in the story are, the focus is not on the people, but is instead on the situation that they are in. These situations can apply to other individuals in different times and places. One such example is the story of Prophet Adam's two sons.[2] The third category is that of more general historical stories. Here, Allah does not identify whom the people in the story are and does not tell us the time period that the story took place in. The story could have occurred in any place or time period. The story is focused on describing the people's situations and the consequences that result from their actions. One such example is the story of the two men, one of whom was given two gardens.[3]

Prophet Muhammad *saaw* also used to tell meaningful stories to his companions and followers. He used true stories about believers from earlier eras to teach Muslims that the hardships that they faced were experienced by believers across different times. These stories served to ease the Muslims' pain of feeling oppressed and persecuted and to increase

---

1. "Program of Islamic *Tarbiyah*", Dr. Muhammad Qutb
2. (Q5, V27-31)
3. (Q18, V32-43)

their patience and perseverance. An example of these stories is the story of the boy and the magician.[4]

Stories in the *Qur'an* and *Seerah* always tell the absolute truth and have many benefits for those who think and reflect as indicated in the following verses from the *Qur'an*:

> "Indeed, in the stories of the prophets there is a lesson '*E'brah*' for those who are endowed with insight, with deep understanding, '*Olel-Albaab*.' This revelation could not possibly be a discourse invented by man: nay indeed, it is a divine revelation confirming the truth of whatever still remains of earlier revelations, clearly spelling out everything and offering guidance and grace unto people who will believe."[5]

> "Certainly, this is the true narrative (about the story of Isa) and Allah is the all Mighty, the all Wise"[6]

> "We narrate unto you their story with truth. Truly, they were young men who believed in their Lord (Allah) and We increased them in guidance"[7]

In the *Qur'an*, Allah *swt* tells us stories for many benefits. The following are a few of those benefits:

• To educate us about the nature of human beings and the social laws set by Allah *swt* the Almighty.

• To correct wrong concepts, attitudes, and behaviors.

• To teach us lessons about the consequences of our own actions and choices

• To encourage and inspire us when we are going through rough times so we can be strong and patient

---

4. Muslim
5. (Q12, V111)
6. (Q3, V62)

Why Storytelling Works

Storytelling is a wonderful tool to help parents and educators teach children concepts, values, and new behaviors. Stories are different than direct instruction or lecturing, because listeners feel safe from criticism and so do not become defensive about being directed, allowing them to learn from the experiences of the characters. They are effective because listeners see themselves in the stories' characters, which makes them better able to relate to the events and feelings that are being projected through the characters. This is particularly true for young children, as they have immense imaginations.

And the Best Stories are . . .

Qur'an and *Seerah* are, of course, the best sources for teaching beliefs, values, and morals. Some other sources for stories that parents should make use of are listed below.
• Stories told by Prophet Muhammad *saaw* to teach Muslims certain values[8]
• Stories about the various stages of Prophet Muhammad's, *saaw*, life
• Islamic history
• The lives of the companions of the prophet, *saaw*, and those who came immediately after them.[9]

We should all use these sources to help us teach our children the important values that they need throughout their lives and as a source of strength and inspiration.

---

8. Check various collections of *Hadeeth* for many stories told by Prophet Muhammad *SAAW*, for example, the story of the man who killed 99 persons and was seeking repentance, etc.
9. As an example, see "The Successor of the Messenger" and "Men Around the Messenger" by Khaled Muhammad Khaled.

Children's Reflections

I "would like to share this reflection of how some children viewed story-telling as a way of *tarbiyah* at a later stage of their life, and how they felt that storytelling had a great impact on forming their personalities:

• One of my fondest memories from my childhood was the story-telling "sessions" I spent with my parents. They could happen at any time of day (or night, for that matter). They served to educate, as well as amuse, and they did this quite well. When it comes to my knowledge of the life of the prophet *saaw*, I can attribute the vast majority of it to the stories told to me as a child; likewise it is for my knowledge of all the other prophets, peace be upon them. As for the amusement I got from the other stories, this has also had a great impact on me, even if in a more implicit manner. When parents try to raise strong, responsible children, the latter often have to stand up in the face of opposition at a time when they are still developing and therefore are very vulnerable. The time the children spend with their parents during this period is usually the main source of support. The storytelling, in this case, is a chance not only to bond with their parents, but also to relieve the stress of the serious situations both the children and the parents must face. It is very useful because it gives the children a chance to see their parents as a source of fun and amusement, not just as a disciplining source. In the end, of course, it is a balance of these techniques that matter. Even now, as an adult, I still enjoy listening to stories from my parents and this shows how similar children and adults sometimes are."

• Storytelling is an effective way of teaching children a lesson. Children will listen patiently and pay attention to a story and they will remember it a lot better than a lecture about behavior. Of course, a story alone will not teach them to behave. The story should act as a way of teaching them morals. Then there should be consequences to their actions if they disobey the moral taught.

No doubt that I loved the storytelling time that my parents spent with me more than anything else. I always eagerly waited for it as a highlight in my day. Whenever they were busy or didn't have the time to tell me a story I felt that I was missing a very important part of my day, until I had the chance to spend time with them again in another storytelling session."[10]

The Purpose of This Book

Because of all the benefits of storytelling as a tool for *tarbiyah*, this book aims to make it easier for you to use this tool effectively by giving you the know-how of story-telling as well as providing a number of stories for you to tell your children.

Through the parenting workshops that my parents gave, it became apparent that there is a need for Islamic stories to correct common misbehaviors and teach Islamic concepts. The aim of this book is to begin to fill that need, *insha' a* Allah.

In the next section, you will learn some tips that will help you make storytelling time fun and relevant for your children. You will also learn some very important techniques to make the stories effective in their lessons.

The Stories

In the rest of this book, you will find stories to correct certain common problems that are regularly faced by parents with their children such as lying, staying up late, complaining that they have no friends, etc.

These stories will also be of assistance in instilling certain morals and Islamic concepts in your child such as:
• Patience
• Gratefulness
• Having a positive outlook toward life

---

10. *Meeting the Challenge of Parenting in the West*, Dr. Ekram Beshir & Dr. Mohamed Rida Beshir, Ch. 4

- The use of *dua*
- That Allah knows and sees everything
- Honesty
- Etc.

An Important Note

I highly recommend that you read the next chapter thoroughly as the success of your storytelling experience will depend largely on applying the principles it teaches.

Chapter 2:
How to Make This Book Work For You & Your Children

Make sure that you read these sections before telling your children the story, as they provide insight into the many possible uses of each story

Your Guide to Each Story

After each story in this book, you will find these headings (if they apply to that story) and notes under each one of them.

• Suggested Age Group:

This is the age group that the story is written for. If your child is outside of this age group, but you think that s/he would enjoy it, it is always up to your discretion. Each child is different and goes through different stages at different times.

• Behaviors Addressed:

Under this heading comes the main problem that the story deals with. It is the focus of the story.

• Behaviors Modeled:
For Children

Here, I list all sorts of good behaviors that are modeled through the characters in the story. This list is sometimes long

What you should do:

– Choose one or two behaviors from the list and hint at them while you tell the story, making comments such as "Oh – *Masha'a* Allah, he helps his Mom set the table." Or "What a good girl she is, she says her *dua* before she eats."

– The next time you tell the story to your children, choose another two points that you want to emphasize, depending on your child's needs.

What you should not do:

– Don't list the lessons explicitly, before, during, or after the story. Don't say something like "What can we learn from this? Well, he always said his *dua*. And he listened to his parents. And he was helpful. And he shared with his sister. And he did his chores. You should be a good boy and do all those things too."

    – Don't make the story into a series of lessons or it will lose its appeal and your children will lose interest.

    As Ibn Mas'ud *raa* narrated, Prophet Muhammad *saaw* used to fear boring the companions and so he adopted a method of brevity in preaching to them[11]

    – Don't try to address all of the behaviors modeled and concepts presented in one telling of the story. Choose a maximum of two to address and even then, hint lightly at them as you go through the story.

For Parents

Here, I list recommended parenting behaviors that are acted out by the parents in the stories. This is purely for your benefit as a parent, so that you can have a better idea of specific parenting principles and what they look like in real life. Your children do not need to hear about this at all.

• Concepts Presented

These are a list of Islamic and moral concepts that are presented in the story. Some of them are explicitly stated in the story, while others are implicit.

What you should do:

    – Choose one and hint at it during the story when the time is appropriate.

    – Between the Behaviors Modeled and the Concepts Presented, choose two that you will hint at during one storytelling setting. Remember, you can always address others next time you tell the story.

What you should not do:

    – As with the Behaviors Modeled, do not explicitly list the concepts presented in the form of lessons, otherwise this will detract from your child's interest in the stories.

---

11. Agreed Upon, Muslim, Bukhari

Recommended Use of This Book

Don't Read, Storytell

The stories in this book were written with the intention that they be read and retold by the parents, not read directly to the children. So, you would read the story first on your own and then at a later time, tell the story to your children.

The stories are written in detail only to serve as examples of the detail that you should tell your story with and other techniques you can use to make the story interesting (e.g. repetition, humour, emotions, etc.) It is not intended that you are going to learn the details and retell them when you retell the story. Just learn the main events in the story and add in your own details as you go.

This may seem strange at first, because we are used to reading books to our children, not telling them stories. You may be afraid that you won't remember the story, but just remember that many, many cultures around the world have rich oral storytelling traditions. You probably know several stories off by heart yourself and could retell them. The storytelling tradition has many benefits for both you and your children.

Storytelling vs. Reading a Book

These are two very different activities and each fulfills different needs than the other.[12] Each of these activities has its own benefits.

Benefits of Storytelling

There are many benefits to storytelling.[13] Below are a few:

• **Bonding**
– Eye contact
– Face to Face
– Your own personality comes through

---

12. "Tell Me a Story: Creating Bedtime Tales Your Children Will Dream On", Chase Collins
13. "Tell Me a Story: Creating Bedtime Tales Your Children Will Dream On", Chase Collins

• **Limitless**
– Your children's imagination and your animation set the tone and make the story more personal and suitable for you
– Relating: Your children imagine the pictures to go along with your description. They will imagine characters, places, and activities that are based on their lives. This makes them relate more easily to the story.
– Freedom: they and you are not limited to the words in the book or the pictures in the story. Your own imaginations can make the story more interesting and applicable to you.
– Customization: You can customize the story to make it more effective for your child.

HOW TO BOND OVER STORYTELLING

• **Setting**
– Sit close to your children
– Cuddle
– Choose a comfortable, cozy place, e.g.. parent's bed, children's bed, a comfy couch

• **Mood**
– Relaxed, not rushed
– Enjoyable
– Sharing and listening

• **Involving your children**
– Look for situations in the story where you can make your children laugh and tickle them
– At repetitive parts in the story, encourage your children to join in and say the parts with you
– If your children interrupt the story to share an experience or ask questions, allow them. Listen attentively – this may be when your children will open up to you about problems that they are facing. Don't tell them to wait until the story is finished.

• **Beginning and Ending the Story**
– If you have a traditional way of beginning and ending a story in your culture or language, use it regularly.

How to Keep it Interesting

• **Voice**
– Exaggerate your voice expressions.
– Change the volume of your voice at different parts of the story according to the events and emotions that are being presented.
– Make different voices for different characters, e.g., use different voices for the parents than for the little kids
– Make funny voices when appropriate.
– Make animal sounds and voices, e.g., when an animal is speaking, make a funny voice and imitate their animal sounds throughout.
– Change the speed of your speech at different parts of the story according to the events and emotions that are being presented.
– Let the emotions presented in the story guide your tone, e.g., at a sad part, slow down and lower your voice. At an exciting part, use a louder voice. At a scary part, speed up and use a louder voice, etc.

• **Facial Expressions & Body Language**
– Use exaggerated facial expressions.
– Whenever there are emotions involved, use your face and your body to express them.
– Don't be scared to overdo it; remember you are replacing the pictures in a book and the Television screen in a show.
– When there is a game or an action involved, use your entire body to imitate it.
– If there is a repetitive action that happens again and again, you can develop an action for it and you and your children can do that action every time it comes up in the story.

How to Customize Your Story

Customizing your story will make it more relevant and effective for your children. People tend to learn more from a model that they perceive as similar to them.[14]

What to Change

• **Gender:** If the main character is a boy, but you are reading to your daughter, make the main character a girl. And vice versa.

• **Games & Activities:** If the child in the story has a hobby or a game that they play and your child does not play this game, you can replace the activity in the story with an activity that your child sometimes plays.

• **Age:** If the child in the story is five years old, but you are telling the story to a seven year old, then make the child six or seven. Only do this if the story will still work with a different age (most do.)

• **What your children call you:** In all the stories, the children call their parents Mom and Dad. Make the child in the story use the labels that your child calls you. E.g. Mom, *Hoyoo, Abee,* Papa, etc.

• **Names of School Friends:** The names of the children's school friends vary in these stories. If your children go to a public school with non-Muslims and Muslims, make sure you include non-Muslim and Muslim names for the characters' friends at school. If your children go to an Islamic school, change the names to make them Muslim names, so that it is more similar to their experiences.

• **Setting:** If possible make the house more similar to yours so that your children can easily imagine it. For example, if you do not have stairs, remove the stairs from the story, etc.

What Not to Change

• **The character's name to your child's name**: Do NOT change the name of the main character to your child's name or to that of a close friend of theirs. If the character's name happens to be your child's name, change it to another name.

14. "Social Psychology", David G. Myers

• **The character's teacher/school to your child's:** Do NOT name the school the same name as your child's school or the teacher the same name as your child's teacher or the best friends the same name as your child's close friends.

• **Situation:** Do not change the situation to make it exactly like yours. If your children see that there are too many similarities between the characters and them, they may feel defensive and resent the story.

Consequences in the Story

The parenting trend in our society at the moment is not to scare children. This trend, I believe, is a good thing for children as they learn to feel more secure and confident.

At the same time, I believe that there needs to be a balance. To frighten children through the consequences that happen to a character in a story while the children themselves are safe and sound in order to change behaviors that could be harmful to the children is beneficial as long as the consequences are not too drastic, like death, as to traumatize the children.

Children also should not be raised so naively as to think that there are no dangers in the world. On the contrary, they need to learn that there are dangers in the world and that everyone is responsible for their own safety. If we neglect or ignore this completely, then we risk raising children who think that the world is completely safe and are not able to judge and avoid dangers and dangerous behaviors [15] Ironically, when we go to this extreme, we put children in danger because of our own fear of scaring them.

How to Remind During & After the Story

While telling the story

• Make sure that you comment about the character's bad behaviors while they are happening. Say things like "This is very wrong.", "How could they do such a thing?", "Oh, that's very bad."

---

15. "Social Psychology", David G. Myers

• Although the story will show and explain this by the end, don't wait until the end to point out which behaviors are wrong.

• This way, your child will not associate the bad behaviors with being fun and glamorous.

After the Story

Later, after you have told your children the story, if they display the behavior that the story addressed, try the following ways of responding.

• Remind them of the story and the character. Say "Do you remember Mustafa when he jumped on the furniture and got hurt. You're not like him. You're a good boy." Or say "Remember how Mustafa learned not to jump on the furniture. You, *masha'a* Allah, you've already learned that! You're a good boy."

• Always make your child out to be a "good boy" or "good girl."

• Never make your child out to be a "bad boy" or "bad girl."

• DO NOT say "Now you're just like that bad boy Mustafa, who jumped on the furniture. Didn't you learn your lesson from him?"

The Bottom Line

• Read the story ahead of time and become familiar with it.

• Tell your children the story, customized for them.

• Be emotionally involved.

• Don't panic or worry if you change the events a little as long as you
  – keep the length of the story similar to build interest and suspense.
  – keep the main points the same.
  – keep the problem and the consequences the same.

• If you are very worried about remembering the order of events then write very short jot notes for yourself of the main ideas or main events in the story. That way, you can glance at it if you need to.

• The eye contact, your interaction, bonding, and the personal touch of your storytelling is more important to your children than it is for you to know the story exactly as it is. Remember, your children never read the story. They won't know if you change it.

Ameenah's Cake

Once upon a time, there was a little girl named Ameenah. She was four years old and her biggest dream was to learn how to ride her bike. One morning, when Ameenah woke up, she saw her father standing at her door.

"*Assalaamu alaikum* Ameeanah, good morning," her father said.

"*Wa' alaikum assalaam.*" Ameenah answered and then she said her waking up *dua*. "*Ashhadu an laa ilaaha illa* Allah, *wa ashhadu anna Muhammadan rasool* Allah."[16]

"I have a surprise for you downstairs."

Ameenah jumped out of bed and ran out the door and down the stairs. Her mother was waiting for her downstairs. "*Assalaamu alaikum* Mom. Where's my surprise?" Ameenah asked.

"Well . . . " her mother said.

"Ameenah, Ameenah," called her father. "Why don't you come on out into the backyard? There's something waiting for you here."

Ameenah ran out into the yard and there it was. A nice new blue bike was waiting for her! It was gorgeous!

"Wow, *masha'a* Allah," said Ameenah. "It's beautiful! I love it!"

"Well come on over here and try it out," her dad suggested. Ameenah walked over and climbed up onto the bicycle.

"*Masha'a* Allah," her mother exclaimed. It's exactly your size! This is terrific." She came over and gave her a big hug.

"Well," said her dad, "congratulations on your new bike."

"Can you teach me to ride it?" asked Ameenah.

---

16. I bear witness that there is no God but Allah, and that Muhammad is the messenger of Allah.

"Not now," answered her father. "First you have to change and have breakfast. Then we can go out for a ride."

"Come on," said her mother.

Ameenah went up to her room and changed her clothes. Then her mother helped her brush her teeth.

"Now I just have to eat breakfast and then I'll be ready to go out on my new bike," Ameenah said excitedly.

"Come sit at the table Ameenah. Your pancake is ready." Ameenah's mom told her.

Ameenah sat down on the chair and said "*Bismillah Ar-rahmaan Ar-rahim*" She took a big piece of her pancake and soaked it in syrup. "Mmmm . . . this is really tasty. Thank you Mommy."

"You're welcome honey," her mom answered.

"*Assalaamu alaikum* Omar," Ameenah said to her little brother. Omar had just crawled into the kitchen, but then he changed his mind and turned around. He started crawling out of the kitchen.

"Omar, Omar," Ameenah called. Then she picked up her plate and fork and went out after Omar.

"Ameenah," her mother called. "Sit down while you eat."

"I'm just seeing Omar, Mom," Ameenah said.

"It doesn't matter. You could drop the plate and it could break and then someone could get hurt. Come here and sit down, Ameenah."

"But Mom, I'm holding the plate really well," Ameenah answered.

"Ameenah, come take a seat," her mother called again.

"Fine," Ameenah said coming back into the kitchen. She sat down at the table with her plate and fork.

Now Ameenah's father came into the kitchen. Ameenah's mom and dad both sat down at the table to eat their pancakes.

"So Ameenah," her father said. "I'm really excited about teaching you how to ride your new bike. We're going to have a lot of fun."

"Yeah, I can't wait," Ameenah said.

Just as Ameenah's parents were saying *Bismillah*, Ameenah saw something outside the window. With her plate in one hand and her fork in the other, Ameenah ran to the window to get a better look.

"Ameenah," her father warned. "Didn't we say that you should always stay seated until you finish eating? Come back here and sit down please."

"Daddy, look!" Ameenah pointed out the window. "There are two orange birds on top of the neighbour's house. Isn't that funny?" Ameenah ate another piece of her pancake and laughed at the funny birds.

"Ameenah," her mom said. "Did you hear what Daddy said? Bring your food and come sit down please."

Ameenah put the last pancake piece into her mouth and then ran back to the table. She put the plate down on the table and announced, "All done! Come on, let's go so you can teach me to ride my bike."

"Ameenah, you should have stayed at the table when you were eating. Next time, sit down at the table until you finish your food, okay?"

"Okay, I will," Ameenah agreed. "Come on, Dad." She said, running out to the backyard.

With her father holding her bike steady, Ameenah climbed onto the bike.

"*Bismillah Ar-rahmaan Ar-rahim*," Ameena said. "I hope I don't fall off the bike."

"Don't worry Ameenah. You said *Bismillah* and Allah will protect you."

With her father behind her, holding onto the seat of her bike, Ameenah started pedaling. She pedaled out of the backyard and onto the sidewalk.

"Daddy, are you there?" Ameenah asked. She was a little bit afraid that he would let go of the bike and then maybe she would fall.

"I'm right here, holding onto your seat," her father answered.

Phew! That was a relief.

Ameenah concentrated very hard on biking. She pedaled and pedaled and before she knew it she had pedaled past her house. Ameenah pedaled and pedaled and she pedaled past her neighbour's house.

"Daddy, are you there?" Ameenah asked in a scared, little voice.

"I'm right here," answered her dad. "You're doing a great job. Just keep pedaling."

So Ameenah did pedal and she pedaled right past another house. Then she pedaled past another house and another house and another house!

"Look Daddy! Look!" Ameenah said. "I biked past all those houses."

"Yes you did! Good for you!" her dad said.

"Daddy, are you still there?" Ameenah asked.

"Yes I am. You just keep pedaling Ameenah," her father told her.

So Ameenah just kept pedaling. She pedaled past one house. Then she pedaled past the second house . . . . Then she even pedaled past the third house.

"Daddy, are you still there?" Ameenah asked.

"Yes," her father answered.

Now Ameenah pedaled faster and faster. She pedaled past another house, then another, and then another. She was going so fast – she felt as if she were flying! She loved biking!

"Daddy, are you still there?" Ameenah yelled over the wind. But there was no answer. "Daddy? Daddy?" Ameenah called out. But . . . there was still no answer. Then all of a sudden, Ameenah saw her dad – he was running beside her. He had let go of the bike! Ameenah was biking all by herself. She loved biking!

She biked up the street and down the street and up the street and down the street. Then she biked all the way home. Ameenah was really hungry from all that biking. Her mom made her a sandwich and put it on a plate on the kitchen table.

"Come and sit down so you can eat Ameenah," her mom called.

Ameenah was so hungry! She ran into the kitchen and sat down on her chair. "*Bismillah*," she said aloud. Then she took a big bite of her sandwich.

"Mmmm . . ." Ameenah said. "*Jazaki Allahu khairan* Mommy. This is good!"

"*Jazana wa iyakum,*" her mom answered. "Ameenah, I have to check where Omar is. I'll be right back. You stay at the table and finish your food, okay?"

"Okay," Ameenah agreed.

Now Ameenah was all alone in the kitchen. She took another big bite of her sandwich and chewed and then she swallowed. Then Ameenah took another bite and she chewed and chewed . . . .

"This is boring," Ameenah thought. "I'm going to play with my dolls while I eat."

Ameenah picked up her plate and walked out of the kitchen. She went to the family room and started playing with her dolls as she ate her sandwich.

"Ameenah!"

Ameenah looked up. Her mom was standing in the doorway looking angry.

"Ameenah, I told you to stay at the kitchen table while you ate. Now look at the mess you've made! This room is full of crumbs," her mom said. "Take your sandwich and go back to the kitchen."

Ameenah felt bad. She didn't mean to upset her mom and she didn't mean to make a mess in the family room. It's just that eating at the table was so boring.

The next day, Ameenah went biking again. This time, she was even better than before. She could bike all by herself and her dad taught her how to turn around on the bike! All the neighbours told her that she was a great biker and she came home feeling wonderful!

"Mommy, mommy – Mrs. Baker says that I'm a great biker!" Ameenah said as she came into the house.

"That's wonderful Honey," Ameenah's Mom gave her a big hug. "I have some good news for you too, Ameenah."

"Really? What?"

"Well, tonight some guests will be visiting us and we need to make something for desert. And I thought, since you've become such a big girl that you could help me bake a cake."

"Yay! I'd love to, Mommy," Ameenah exclaimed. "Wow, I've never baked before."

"Well, come on," her mother said. "Go wash your hands so we can get started.

Ameenah washed her hands quickly and went into the kitchen. With all the ingredients on the table, Ameenah said "*bismillah*" then they started. First Ameenah put the flour in the bowl. Then she put the sugar in the bowl. Then she even got to pour in a cup of milk. Ameenah counted as her mom put in the eggs.

"One egg . . . Two . . . Three . . . Four – Enough. Now the oil Mom," Ameenah said. She watched her mom pour the oil in. Then came the hard part. Ameenah took a big spoon and started mixing. She mixed and she mixed and she mixed. And she mixed and mixed and mixed. Finally Ameenah's mom said that the batter was ready for the oven. Together they poured the batter into the pan and then Ameenah's mom put it in the oven.

Soon this wonderful chocolate smell came out of the oven and spread to every room in the house.

Ameenah's dad came down the stairs sniffing. Sniff, sniff, sniff, sniff. "Mmmm . . . What is that wonderful smell?" he asked.

"That's Ameenah's chocolate cake," her mother answered. Ameenah took a deep breath. The cake smelt so good. She couldn't wait to eat it! Ameenah waited and waited for the cake to be ready. The smell got yummier and yummier. It got sweeter and more chocolaty and mmmm mmmm – it was just SO good!

Then when Ameenah's mom took the cake out of the oven, the smell got even better! And the cake looked delicious!

"Mommy, can I put the icing on?" asked Ameenah.

"Of course you can. It's your cake. Just wait until the cake cools down, Honey," her mother told her.

And Ameenah waited patiently until the cake was cool. Then her mother handed her a bowl full of icing and showed her how to spread it on the cake.

First Ameenah iced the top of the cake. Then she iced the sides, and before she knew it, the whole cake was covered in icing. "Mmm," said Ameenah's father, "that looks great!"

"You are our new expert baker, Ameenah!" her mother exclaimed. Ameenah felt great. She had just baked a cake and it looked terrific. She wanted to taste it but she knew that she had to wait until the guests came. Ameenah waited for the guests to arrive. She watched the cake. It was so wonderfully chocolaty. It smelt so good. It looked so good. Now she just wanted to taste it.

"Ameenah," her mother called. "The guests have arrived. Come say *assalaamu alaikum*."

Ameenah walked into the living room and greeted all the guests. There were so many of them. "Oh no," she thought to herself. "Maybe the cake is too small. Maybe there are too many people. Oh no, I hope there's enough for everyone. I hope there's enough for me."

Ameenah waited worriedly through the grown-ups' conversations. Then she waited worriedly through dinner. When everyone was finished dinner, the big moment came!

Ameenah's mother walked into the dining room with the cake.

"Ameenah baked this cake," she announced to all the guests.

"Oooh," said Auntie Sumaiyah.

"*Masha'a* Allah!" said Uncle Ahmed.

"It looks great!" exclaimed Auntie Rasheedah.

"Ameenah, Ameenah, Ameenah," said Uncle Yusuf.

"Yes," Ameenah answered.

"You are one wonderful baker!"

Ameenah had a big smile on her face. She was really happy that everyone thought her cake looked so good, but she was still a little worried that there wouldn't be enough for everyone. Ameenah watched her mother serve the cake. She watched and hoped that there would be enough for everyone. There were still three people left to serve . . . now two people left . . . now one person . . . *Alhamdulillah!* The cake was just right. There were exactly enough pieces, not one piece less, not one piece more.

"Okay," Ameenah's mom called out. "All the children will have their cake on the table. I've put your pieces of cake there."

All the children rushed to the table. All of them except for Ameenah. Ameenah stood quietly and watched to see if the grown-ups liked her cake. She watched her mother eat. She watched her father eat. She watched Auntie Sumaiyah eat. She watched Uncle Ahmad eat. She watched Auntie Rasheedah eat and she watched Uncle Yusuf eat. They all looked very happy. They looked like they were enjoying the cake. In fact, they liked it so much that they finished up their pieces right away!

Ameenah looked over at the table. All the kids loved the cake too! They loved it so much that they gobbled it all up. There was only one piece of cake left on the table, Ameenah's piece.

The other children got up, washed their hands, and began playing together.

"Ameenah, aren't you going to eat your cake?" asked Uncle Yusuf.

"Definitely!" Ameenah said. She walked over to the table and picked up her plate. She looked over to where all the children were playing Duck Duck Goose.

"Wait," Ameenah called. "Don't start without me!" Ameenah ran over and CRASH!!!! While she was running, she tripped and fell. The plate slipped from Ameenah's hands and crashed onto the ground. It broke into hundreds and hundreds of little pieces. And her wonderful piece of cake fell too! Ameenah stood back up and stared at the ground. Her piece of cake was all dirty and filled with pieces of her plate. Ameenah's eyes welled up with tears.

"Mommy!" she cried, "I didn't get to taste the cake."

"Ameenah – step back. This is really dangerous."

"But mommy!" Ameenah cried, "Can't I just try a little piece."

"I'm sorry honey, but the cake is full of broken pieces from the plate and it's all dirty too! It's just too dangerous - you can't eat it." Ameenah watched in horror as her mom swept up the cake and threw it out in the garbage. Ameenah ran over to the garbage can and stared at her cake. Tears rolled down her cheek.

"But Mommy, I didn't mean to drop it," Ameenah explained. "I was holding the plate well. I really wanted a piece of my cake."

"I know you didn't mean it Ameenah," her mother said. "It was an accident. But you know, you shouldn't be running around with your food. When you have food, you should stay at the table and that way, *insha'a* Allah, it won't fall. I'm sorry you didn't get to taste your cake, Honey." Ameenah felt terrible – she didn't get to eat from her cake, just because she hadn't sat at the table. She decided that next time she was eating, she would sit at the table until she finished all her food.

*****

SUGGESTED AGE GROUP
3 – 7 years old

BEHAVIORS ADDRESSED
• Not sitting properly while eating their food

BEHAVIORS MODELED
For Children

• To use Islamic phrases regularly,
e.g., *Assalaamu alaikum, Masha'a* Allah, *Jazaakum Allahu khairan*, etc.

• To treat their parents nicely and respectfully

• To say *Bismillah* before they begin anything and to make *dua*

For Parents

• Be affectionate and express love to your children,
e.g., calling them "honey", hugging them, etc.

• Involve your children in your daily activities (e.g., baking)

• Build your children's confidence through
– developing their skills,
e.g., Ameenah's father – biking,
e.g., Ameenah's mother – baking.

• Give lots of encouragement in an exaggerated way that
suits the child's exaggerated emotions.
E.g. when Ameenah's mom says to her father,
"This is Ameenah's chocolate cake."

All My Days are Good

Once upon a time, there was a little boy named Osama who lived with his mom, his dad, and his little sister. Everyday Osama woke up in the morning and went to school. At school, he played with his friends and learned many new things. One day when Osama woke up, he got out of bed and walked over to the curtains. He opened the curtains and looked outside – it was a beautiful sunny day! His mother walked into his room and saw him, awake and out of bed.

"Oh, *Masha'a* Allah," she said. "You're already awake! Well good for you. Have you said your dua?"

"*Ash-hadu an laa ilaha illa Allah, wa anna Muhamadan rasool Allah.*[17] Oh Allah, make my day a good day and protect me from anything harmful throughout my day." Osama was a big boy, and he said the dua all by himself every morning.

"*Insha'a* Allah, you'll have a wonderful day," his mother said, giving him his morning hug and kiss. "Now, go get ready so that you're not late for school."

Osama ran to use the bathroom and brush his teeth. When he came out he saw his mother holding up two different outfits for him to choose from.

"Oh, definitely that one," he said pointing to the blue shirt and blue jeans. After all, blue was his favourite colour. After Osama dressed, and ate breakfast, he was off to school.

At school, Osama did many, many things. In the morning his teacher read a story to the class. The story was all about the different kinds of animals. Osama loved animals.

---

17. I bear witness that there is no God but Allah, and that Muhammad is the messenger of Allah.

"Okay, now three lucky people are going to be painting pictures of the animals that we read about. Now, let's see . . . who will they be today?"

Osama raised his hand high up into the air. He watched his teacher as she looked around the carpet and tried to choose a person. "Our first painter is . . . David," she said. Osama stretched his hand up higher. "Our second painter is Mariam," she said. Osama stretched his hand even higher up in the air. "And our third painter is . . . Osama!"

Osama was so excited. He jumped up singing, "Thank you, thank you, thank you." He walked over to the painting station and there, after putting on his apron, he began his picture. Osama used all sorts of colours and painted all sorts of animals. He painted birds and cats and dogs and giraffes and elephants and tigers and lions and bears. When the picture was finished, Osama told his teacher.

"Well, isn't this a *beautiful* picture," she marveled. "I will hang it up to dry so you can take it home tonight and show it to your parents. They will be so proud." Osama smiled broadly – he was very happy about the picture

Then it was time for everybody to go to the carpet. There the teacher announced, "Okay class we're going to play Duck-Duck-Goose. Who would like to be it?"

Osama raised his hand high in the air. All the other children had their hands up too. The teacher picked Leila. Osama hoped that Leila would pick him.

"Duck, duck, duck," she said. As she came closer, Osama got ready to run. He hoped she would pick him. "Duck," she said as she tapped his head. Osama sighed. Leila picked Andrea and they ran around the circle.

When it was Andrea's turn to pick, Osama hoped she would pick him, but she picked Mohamed instead. Osama really hoped Mohamed would pick him, but Mohamed just passed right by him, saying, "duck" as he tapped his head. Mohamed picked Alan.

Osama hoped that Alan would pick him. "Say goose, say goose," Osama whispered as Alan came closer. "Duck," Alan said as he tapped Osama's head. Alan picked Melissa.

"Pick me, pick me," Osama pointed at himself as Melissa came over, but she picked Safia.

"Safia," Osama whispered to her, "pick me." Safia didn't pick him – she picked Omar.

Osama was getting sadder and sadder. Every time somebody was picked to be it, he hoped they would pick him. And every time, they picked somebody else. The entire game, nobody picked Osama and he never got to be it.

"Alright class," the teacher said after Duck-Duck-Goose, "it's snack time. Everybody wash you're hands and sit down to eat your snacks."

Osama washed his hands and sat down at his table. "Bismillah," he said as he opened up his lunch box. "*Allahuma Baarik lanaa feemaa raza-qtana wa qinaa 'athaaba nar.*"[18] Osama ate half of his cheese sandwich. Then he ate a piece of his nice, juicy apple and drank his juice.

"Snack time is finished, class," his teacher said. "Everybody clean up please."

Osama closed his lunch box and wiped his table clean. He put his lunch box away and went to line up. Osama's class was going outside for playtime. It was Osama's turn to ride the tricycle today and he *loved* riding the tricycle. "*Bismillah*," he said as he climbed up onto the tricycle, and he began pedaling.

First, Osama pedaled slowly past the tree. Then he turned and pedaled past his friends who were playing in the sandbox.

"Hi!" they waved to him. "Hi Osama."

"Hi," Osama called back.

Then he turned and pedaled away from them. He started pedaling faster and faster. Now, Osama felt like he was flying – it was the best feeling in the world. He *loved* biking! Then he turned again and pedaled faster and suddenly – CRASH!!

---

18. In the name of Allah. Oh Allah bless what you have given us, and protect us from the hell fire.

Osama lay on the floor, the tricycle on top of his leg. Osama grabbed his knee. "Owwww!" he cried. "My knee, my knee. Ow ow ow ow. My knee!" Tears rolled down Osama's face. The teacher ran over to him.

"Are you okay, Osama?" she asked pulling the tricycle off of his leg. "What hurts?"

"My knee," Osama cried. "My knee hurts so much!"

"Oh, you got a little scratch," his teacher said. "Come on in and I'll get you a band-aid."

Osama looked down at his knee – he was bleeding! "Owwwwww," Osama cried as he hobbled inside with his teacher. "It hurts!" It hurt when she cleaned it. It hurt when she put the band-aid on. And it hurt when he walked back outside to sit on the bench. "Now, I can't even play," he said to himself as he sat on the bench. "My knee hurts!" Osama sat on the bench and watched the other children play. It wasn't fair.

Osama was happy when it was time to go back inside, because he couldn't play anyway. Inside, Osama sat on the carpet with the rest of the children as the teacher read them all a story. Then they sang their good-bye song and got ready to go home.

That night at home, as Osama's mother tucked him into bed, she gave him a kiss on his forehead. "Well Osama," she said, hugging him close to her, "you've eaten your snack and brushed your teeth and put on your pajamas. You've said 'Good night' and 'assalaamu alaikum' to your dad and your brother and your sister. We've read your story. It's time to say your prayers and go to sleep."

Osama read his *Qur'an*. "*Masha'a* Allah!" his mother smiled. "What a wonderful little *Qur'an* reciter you are! Now thank Allah for giving you a good day."

"But Mom," Osama said, "I didn't have a good day. I had a terrible day!"

"What do you mean Osama? Why do you think you had a terrible day?"

"I told you about when I fell and hurt my knee. That's not good," Osama said.

"That's true," his mother said. "But you only got a little hurt"

"No, it hurt a lot."

"Well Osama, I know that it feels like it hurt a lot, but it was just a little scratch. Allah made sure that you didn't get really hurt and break your leg! That's a good thing."

"That's true," Osama said. "But when we were playing Duck-Duck-Goose, nobody picked me. That's not good."

"I know that that doesn't feel good," his mother said. "But you were a good boy. You were patient and you waited nicely, even though you were sad. You didn't yell and scream or hit the other children. Right?"

"Right."

"Well," his mother said smiling, "then Allah gave you lots and lots of good deeds for being such a good and patient boy. That way, you can go to *Jannah* and there you can have anything you want!"

"That's a good thing," Osama smiled.

"Were there any other things that happened today that you weren't happy about?" his mother asked.

Osama thought about it for a minute. "No."

"Well then, let me remind you of something that happened that you were happy about. Remember when the teacher picked you to paint a picture about the animals?"

"Yeah," Osama grinned, "and when she said my painting was wonderful! And when I brought it home, you said it was terrific!"

"Well Osama, it sounds to me like you had a good day after all," his mother said. "Looks like you have a lot to thank Allah for."

"You're right," Osama said and he put his hands up and began saying his *dua*. "Oh Allah, thank you for giving me a good day. Thank you for making sure that I didn't break my leg when I fell from my bike. And thank you for helping me be good and patient so I could earn good deeds when my friends didn't pick me for Duck-Duck-Goose. And thank you for making my teacher pick me to paint and making everybody like my painting. Thank you, Allah."

Osama's mother gave him a kiss on the cheek. "Oh Allah," she said, "thank you for giving me such a wonderful son like Osama." She gave him a hug and kissed him goodnight. "*Assalaamu alaikum*, Osama," his mother said. "Have a good night."

*****

SUGGESTED AGE GROUP
3 – 7 years old

BEHAVIORS MODELED
For Children
• To say the different duas throughout their day

• Morning routine and Bedtime routine

• To use Islamic phrases regularly,
e.g., *Assalaamu alaikum, Masha'a* Allah, *Jazaakum Allahu khairan*, etc.

For Parents
• Start the day off by showing love and affection to your children and projecting a positive attitude for the day

• Train your children for critical thinking by giving them choices and allowing them to make decisions
E.g. when Osama's mother has him choose his outfit for the day

• Use the incidents that happen in the children's day to teach them Islamic concepts and belief

CONCEPTS ADDRESSED
• The Muslim is rewarded for being patient through hardships and being thankful through times of ease. As the prophet *saaw* said, "I am amazed at the affair of the believer: all his affairs are good for him. And that is not the case for anyone except for the believer. If he goes through a time of ease, he is grateful, and that is good for him. And if he goes through hardships, he is patient, and that is good for him." [Narrated by Muslim.]

• For this reason, believers never have a "terrible day." They should never call a day or a week, "a bad day" or "an awful time," etc. though they may be having a difficult time

• Allah is the protector.

• Allah is the provider (gives us everything)

Playing Alone

Once upon a time, there was a little girl named Fatimah. Fatimah lived with her mother, her father, her two older brothers, her younger sister, and her pet hamster. Fatimah was 6 years old and she had many, many hobbies. She liked to draw and colour. She liked to play with her blocks. She liked to sing songs and tell jokes. At school, Fatimah loved to play games with her friends at recess.

Every day at school, when recess time came, Fatimah went outside with her friends. Everyday they all decided what to play together. And everyday they all played together and Fatimah had a lot of fun. Everyday this happened, until one day when everything changed.

That Monday at recess time, Fatimah was playing hopscotch with her friends.

"Your turn," Amirah said and Fatimah started hopping.

Hop! Hop! Hop! She loved hopscotch. Hop! Hop! Hop! Fatimah hopped all the way back to her friends.

"Your turn, Jessica," she announced.

"Fatimah," said Sarah in a mean voice, "You take too long hopping back and forth – so you can't play anymore!"

"What? But I didn't take too long!" Fatimah protested.

"You did," said Sarah.

"I won't take so long next time then," Fatimah promised.

"There is no next time," Sarah yelled. "I said you're out of the game! Leave! Get out of here! Shoo!"

Fatima looked at Sarah. Her eyes welled up with tears. How could this happen? She walked away slowly, looking back at her friends, watching them hop and play. She wished she wasn't so slow. She wished she could play with them. Fatimah sat on the bench and watched them all recess long.

When Fatimah went home that night she told her mother what happened. She cried as she told the story – it was awful to remember the feeling again.

Fatimah's mother hugged her tightly. "That wasn't very nice of Sarah at all," she said. "I know how much it hurt your feelings."

Fatimah nodded.

"Tomorrow, I think you should take your Frisbee so that you can let the girls play Frisbee with you."

"But what if Sarah won't play with me?" Fatimah asked through her tears.

"Well, even if Sarah doesn't play, it's okay. See if any of the other girls want to play. I'm sure that they'll want to play with you. Now, come on, let's go get the Frisbee."

The next day at recess, Fatimah took her Frisbee out of her backpack and ran out to meet her friends.

"Look what I brought," she said, holding up the Frisbee to show them all. "Who wants to play?"

"Frisbee is a stupid game!" Sarah said. "I'm not playing."

"Amirah? Jessica? Susan? Nancy? Do you want to play?" Fatimah asked meekly.

"No!" Sarah answered. "They're playing tag with me." Sarah tagged Amirah and they all started running. Fatimah stood and watched them. She watched them run and laugh. She wanted to play tag. She ran after them. "I'm playing too," she said as she taunted Jessica, who was it. Jessica ran after her and then she caught her. Now, Fatimah was it! She ran and ran after her friends.

"FATIMAH!" Sarah yelled. "You aren't playing with us! Go away!"

"But Jessica tagged me," Fatimah protested.

"Jessica," Sarah yelled. "Fatimah's not playing. Everybody! Fatimah's not playing! If you run after her or catch her, you won't play either."

"But she's it," Jessica said. "Now who's going to be it?"

"I'm it," announced Sarah.

The girls ran and Sarah ran after them and Fatimah was left standing there all alone. Why didn't her friends like her anymore? Why wouldn't they let her play with them? She stood by the tree and watched them play. She watched them play all recess long.

When Fatimah went home that night, she told her mother and father what happened. "They didn't want to play Frisbee. They all wanted to play tag and they didn't let me play with them. I hate this Frisbee. I just want to play with my friends."

"What did you do for recess then?" her father asked.

"Nothing," Fatimah said sadly.

"Well, you must have done something, Fatimah," her mother said. "Tell us what you did so we can help you find a good way to deal with this problem."

"I just stood there and watched them," she said. "They were playing and having so much fun and I couldn't play with them, so I just watched. I was all alone."

"Hmmm," Fatimah's father thought.

"Hmmm," Fatimah's mother thought.

Fatimah watched her parents think. She wanted to know the answer. She wanted to know what to do.

"I have an idea," her mother said.

"What?" Fatimah asked.

"Well Fatimah, I think you should take your bouncy ball with you to school tomorrow."

"No!" Fatimah said. "The Frisbee didn't work – the bouncy ball won't work either!"

"Fatimah, just listen to the idea first, okay," her father said.

"You're right about the Frisbee, Fatimah," her mother said, "but not about the bouncy ball."

"But what's the difference?" Fatimah asked.

"Well, you can only play with the Frisbee if your friends are playing with you, but the bouncy ball – you can play with it alone."

"Alone?" Fatimah asked, surprised. "I don't want to play alone. I want to play with my friends. Playing alone is no fun!"

"You see Fatimah," her father said. "That's part of the problem. People only want to play with somebody who is having fun. They never want to play with someone who is sad and upset and not having fun."

"So," her mother said, " this is the plan. At recess time tomorrow, take your bouncy ball and see if your friends want to play. If they do, then you can all play with the ball together. If they don't, then you take the ball and play with it alone. And when you're playing with the ball alone, have fun, smile, and laugh."

"Mom, Dad," Fatimah stared at them. "I can't play with the ball alone. What would I do? It'll be so boring!"

"No it won't," her father said. "You can throw it up in the air and catch it. You can bounce it on the ground."

"You can throw it in the air and see if you can clap before it comes back down. You can count how many times you can bounce it in a row," her mother added.

"But, I'll still be alone!" Fatimah exclaimed. "I don't want to play alone!"

"Fatimah," her mother said. "You need to learn to have fun, even if your friends aren't with you."

"Yeah," her father agreed. "Because when your friends look over and they see a sad Fatimah, then they won't want to play with you. But if they look over and see a happy Fatimah, then they'll want to come and play with you. It might not happen right away, but soon enough, they'll figure out that this is a happy Fatimah – and then, they'll want to play with you."

And so Fatimah and her mother and her father found the bouncy ball and put it in her schoolbag. The next day Fatimah went off to school. At recess time, she put the ball in her pocket and went outside. She was walking over to her friends when she saw Sarah staring at her. Sarah said something to the other girls and they all turned and walked away. Fatimah stopped walking. She stood, frozen in her spot, a lump in her throat and tears in her eyes. She watched her friends talking and laughing. She wanted to be with them. Her tears started rolling down her face and she put her hands in her pocket. Suddenly she felt the bouncy ball.

'I don't want to play with the bouncy ball!' she thought. 'I just want to play with my friends!' All recess long she watched her friends and wished she was with them. She walked around with a frown on her face and with her head hung low, staring down at her feet. She missed her friends.

When she went home that night, her parents asked her how the plan had worked.

"It didn't work," she said. "I don't want to play alone! I want to play with my friends."

"Did you try playing with the ball?" her father asked.

"Did you smile and have fun while you were playing?" her mother asked.

"No," said Fatimah with a frown on her face.

"Well," said her mother, "you can't say that it hasn't worked if you haven't even tried it. Tomorrow, take the ball out and play with it, even if you don't feel like it. I know, I know that it's going to work. It might take some time, but Allah will make it work for you, because Allah loves you and you are doing the right thing. Just give it a try!"

"And make sure you try to have fun playing," her father said.

The next day at morning recess Fatimah walked around with her hand in her pocket, holding the ball. She didn't feel like playing with it. She didn't feel like being by herself. She stared at her friends – they were having fun. They were laughing and playing together. She wanted to be with them.

Fatimah was sad. In class, she frowned. She frowned at the teacher. She frowned at the other boys and girls in her class.

Even when it was time to sing Fatimah's favourite song, she just didn't feel like it. She frowned through the song and she barely whispered the words.

When it was time for craft, Fatimah was still sad. Even though the teacher showed them how to make a bunny rabbit from cotton balls, Fatimah sat there frowning. She didn't really want to make her bunny rabbit. So she frowned as she made the bunny rabbit and she complained.

"This is so hard," she said. "And the glue won't stick! I hate making bunny rabbits!"

At lunchtime, Fatimah was still sad. She looked at her lunch and she frowned. She ate her sandwich and she frowned and she complained.

"This bread doesn't taste good," she complained. "And I don't like apple juice!"

At lunch recess, Fatimah watched her friends play. She wanted to play with them. She walked around, frowning and angry. She felt the ball in her pocket. She didn't want to play ball – she wanted to play with her friends. All recess long, she watched them play – they were having a good time. She was having a terrible time.

After lunch, it was reading time. Fatimah was still sad. She tried to read her book, but she was so upset that she just complained.

"This book is so boring," she complained to Amirah while Amirah tried to read. "I hate reading!"

When it was time for gym, Fatimah was still sad. Even though they were playing Fatimah's favourite game, dodge ball, Fatimah still frowned and complained.

"Nobody is throwing the ball to me," she complained to Jessica. "I hate dodge ball!"

Then it was time for afternoon recess. Fatimah went outside and looked over at her friends: Sarah and Amirah and Jessica and Susan and Nancy. They were holding hands and skipping up and down the playground. She wanted to hold their hands. She wanted to skip. She wanted to play with them, but they wouldn't let her!

She walked around, frowning. She watched them sing and skip. She stuck her hands in her pockets and there was the ball again.

The bouncy ball . . . . When she got home tonight her parents would ask her about that. She hadn't played with it at all and then they'll say that she can't say it didn't work if she didn't give it a chance.

'It won't work anyway,' she thought. 'I know it won't, but Mom and Dad don't know. I'll try it, just so I can tell them.'

She took the ball out of her pocket and looked at it. She would rather be with her friends. She threw it up in the air once and caught it. She looked over at her friends. They weren't even looking at her. She frowned. She threw it up in the air again and caught it. This was boring. She threw it up in the air again and caught it. Then she threw it on the ground and bounced it once. She looked over at her friends, they were still skipping and singing and having fun – they didn't care if she was playing with a bouncy ball or not. Fatimah frowned even more– she hated the bouncy ball. The plan didn't work!

At home that night, Fatimah's parents asked her about the plan.

"It didn't work," she whined.

"Did you play with the bouncy ball?" her father asked.

"Yeah, a little," Fatimah answered.

"Did you have fun when you were playing?" her mother asked.

"No – it was so boring. And my friends were holding hands and skip-ping! I wanted to be with them. The bouncy ball was no fun at all!"

"Well then you didn't really try the plan, Fatimah" her mother said.

"Fatimah, you have to play with the ball a lot," her father explained. "You can't give up after just a little. And you need to have fun when you're playing. If you're not having fun, then no one else will want to come play with you."

Fatimah didn't know if it would work. Nobody wanted to play with her and all she wanted was to play with her friends.

Then, the next day at school, something amazing happened. Before school, Fatimah needed to go to the bathroom. Fatimah got a hall pass and went inside to the bathroom. She went into a stall and closed the door. Just then, she heard two girls come in. She heard their voices and she knew who they were: it was Jessica and Amirah! And they were talking about her!

"I don't know what's wrong with Fatimah," Amirah said. "She's just not the same anymore."

"Yeah," Jessica agreed. "She used to be so happy and cheerful. Now she's always sad and frowning. And all she ever does is complain!"

"Exactly!" Amirah agreed. "Yesterday when we were reading, she just complained about her book!"

"And at gym, when we were playing dodge ball, she just complained about that," Jessica added.

"It's no fun to be around her anymore, because all she ever does is complain" Amirah said.

"Yeah," Jessica agreed.

Jessica and Amirah walked out of the bathroom then. Fatimah came out of the stall and looked at herself in the mirror. It was true – they were right! She looked sad and she was frowning! And she did complain too much now. Her parents were right – nobody liked to play with someone who's sad and upset all the time. Nobody likes to play with someone who's not having fun! Fatimah looked at herself in the mirror again – she had a plan. She touched the bouncy ball in her pocket. Then she smiled and walked out of the bathroom.

At recess time, Fatimah took out her bouncy ball and bounced it. She laughed and sang to herself while she played. She looked over at her friends – they were playing tag and they weren't even looking at her. She felt sad and she wanted to stop playing.

'No,' she thought to herself. 'You can't give up. You can have fun playing alone. It's just hard to get used to, but you have to keep trying.'

And so Fatimah kept trying. She played and played and laughed and sang. All recess long, Fatimah played alone.

After recess, in class – it was time for colouring. Usually Fatimah loved colouring, but today as she looked over at Sarah who was sharing her markers with her friends, Fatimah felt sad. She didn't feel like smiling.

'No,' she thought to herself. 'You can't give up. You can have fun colouring alone. It's just hard to get used to, but you have to keep trying.'

And so Fatimah put a smile on her face and coloured the picture. She tried not to think about Sarah and her markers and her friends. She started singing to herself as she coloured and she concentrated hard on not going outside the lines.

When Amirah looked up and asked her if she could borrow her blue, Fatimah said "Sure," in the most cheerful voice she could.

At lunchtime, Fatimah felt sad, as she saw her friends talking together. She felt like frowning and complaining.

'No,' she thought to herself. 'You can't give up. You can have fun eating lunch alone. It's just hard to get used to, but you have to keep trying.'

Fatimah thought of what she could do to have fun. She couldn't sing while she was eating. She couldn't play with the bouncy ball inside. Her mom and dad had said to play even when she was alone, to do something fun and have fun doing it. She had an idea. She took out a piece of paper and a pencil and she began to draw a picture. As she ate her lunch, she drew one picture after another. It was fun and it kept her busy.

At lunch recess, Fatimah took out her ball again. And she played alone again. And she smiled and laughed again.

At afternoon recess, Fatimah took out her ball again. And she played alone again. And she smiled and laughed again. But in her mind, Fatimah wondered if this would ever work. She had been playing alone all day long. She had been laughing and smiling even though she felt sad. None of her friends had come to play with her.

At home, Fatimah told her parents what happened. She told them how hard she had tried, but that no one had played with her all day long.

"I know it's hard," her mother said, "but you need to keep trying. And have fun. Don't always look over at the other girls. Let yourself enjoy your game."

"We're really proud of you," her father said. "We know this isn't easy, but you just kept trying. Allah will help you, because you're doing the right thing. And tomorrow, we know you'll be able to do it again."

The next day, Fatimah took her bouncy ball to school again and at recess time she played alone with it again. This time, Fatimah, did her best not to look over at her friends. She threw the ball up in the air and clapped to see how many times she could clap before she had to catch the ball. It was a fun game, but Fatimah was still lonely.

In class, as she put the ball in her desk, Amirah asked, "What is that green thing in your desk?"

"It's my bouncy ball," Fatimah said cheerfully. "It's so much fun to play with. We can play with it at recess if you want."

"It looks neat," Amirah said.

And then they got down to work, doing their math.

At lunch recess, Fatimah ran and bounced her bouncy ball all around the yard. She passed her friends once and none of them said anything to her. She passed them again, this time, she waved happily and Amirah and Jessica waved back. The third time she passed them, Amirah and Jessica ran after her.

"Can we play with you?" they asked.

"Sure," Fatimah threw the ball to Jessica. Jessica caught it and bounced it once. Then she threw it to Amirah, who caught it and bounced it once. Then she threw it to Fatimah, who caught it and bounced it once.

Fatimah saw that Sarah and Susan and Nancy were all watching them play. "Do you want to play?" she called out.

"No!" Sarah exclaimed. "It's such a stupid game."

Fatimah felt mad. She wanted to stop playing and cry. She wanted to yell at Sarah. Then she remembered what her parents had said. She remembered what Jessica and Amirah had said in the bathroom. Nobody

wants to play with someone who's upset. People want to play with someone who's having fun.

Fatimah smiled and said, "Your choice," in a cheerful voice. Then she
threw the ball to Jessica.

Sarah and Susan and Nancy walked away. For the rest of recess time,
Jessica and Amirah played with Fatimah and her bouncy ball. And they
all had fun, laughing and cheering as they bounced and threw the ball.

The next recess Amirah and Jessica played with Fatimah again. First
they played with her bouncy ball and then, when they got bored, they all
played tag together.

That night Fatimah told her parents exactly what happened.

"So I got to play with Amirah and Jessica," she said "and it was lots
of fun. But Sarah and Susan and Nancy still didn't play with me. And
Sarah even said it was a stupid game."

"You know, Fatimah," her father said. "Sometimes, some people act
mean. And when they do that, you don't need them to play with you. If
Sarah is being mean, never mind her. Play with the other girls and don't
worry about Sarah."

"Yeah," her mother agreed. "If she decides to be nice and wants to
play, you can play with her. But if she stays this way, then just ignore her
and have fun playing with the others or on your own."

"And remember," her father said. "If you find yourself playing alone
tomorrow or the day after or next week or any time at all, don't be sad.
Play your game and have fun."

"You can have fun playing alone," her mother said.

Fatimah smiled. She had learned her lesson. Maybe it wasn't easy
playing alone, but it sure was better than just standing around and frowning when she was alone. From that day on, Fatimah smiled and played
and was cheerful, whether she was alone or with her friends.

*****

SUGGESTED AGE GROUP

5 – 8 years old

BEHAVIORS ADDRESSED

• The complaint "Nobody wants to play with me."

BEHAVIORS MODELED

For Children

• To keep trying even when they don't feel like it and be persistent in order to improve their situation
• To be cheerful and positive even when things are hard
• To ask their parents for advice and try out their suggestions
• To try to find solutions for problems that they face
• Not to sulk and complain and behave based on feeling sorry for themselves
• Not to lose their temper when others are mean to them
• Not to hold a grudge (e.g., Fatimah toward her friends)

For Parents

• Listen, empathize and comfort your children. Then move on to give suggestions for the problem and to project a positive outlook to give your children hope
• Help your children look for a solution, but don't blame them or undermine their abilities, e.g., Don't say "Why didn't you do . . . ?" "You shouldn't have let . . . "Because your child feels rejected by their friends, if they sense blame from you, they will take it as rejection. This will limit their ability to try solutions and will damage their confidence
• Show your children understanding, empathy, and contain your own emotions, hurt, and anger
• Be patient while your children are sorting out their frustration and their feelings and sorting through the different possible solutions, e.g., when Fatima rejected her mother's bouncy ball idea

• Understand that the children's emotions will take a while and they need to go through different emotional stages in order to come around and experience for themselves what their parents are telling them. Children need that time and that experience for their feelings to change and for them to be ready to try out the suggestions that their parents give them

• Do NOT get angry with them for not trying your suggestions. Instead, continue to encourage and support them. This will help your children to eventually try your suggestions and, later, to learn to think of their own solutions for new problems that they face

• Talk with your children about their day

• Follow up closely with your child on their problem, e.g., Fatimah's parents checked everyday how the plan had gone and when she said it didn't work, they pressed for details and learned more from her

• Put faith and confidence in the children even when they are not able to do it yet, e.g., "I know you can do it."

CONCEPTS PRESENTED

• You can always do something to improve the situation

• To improve any situation, you need to work on it and be patient, because change takes time

• Have faith and trust in Allah that He will help those who do good, try their best, and do all they can to improve the situation

• "The good deed and the evil deed are not alike. Repel the evil deed with one which is better, then lo! he, between whom and thee there was enmity (will become) as though he was a bosom friend."[19]

• Look after yourself, but don't sink to bad behavior like the person who's aggressing on you

---

19. (Q 41, v34)

Mahmood's Trip

Once upon a time, there was a little boy named Mahmood. Mahmood was seven years old and he lived with his mother, his father, and his five-year-old sister Zainab. Now Mahmood and Zainab were both very, very, very excited because something very special was about to happen. It was the last week of school and soon it would be summer vacation. Because Mahmood and Zainab had been very good all year long, because they had done their homework every day, and they had made their beds and tidied their rooms and set the table for dinner everyday, their parents had a big treat for them. They were taking them to Fun World on the first day of summer vacation.

Fun World was a big theme park with all sorts of really exciting rides. It had a Ferris wheel, Bumper cars, Spinning Cups, Busy Boats, Pony Rides, Swinging Birds, and best of all it had the Dragon Ride.

Mahmood and Zainab were very excited about going to Fun World. They were so excited about it that it was all they talked about. They talked about it at breakfast time. They talked about it on their bus ride to school. They talked about it with their teacher and their friends in class. They talked about it on their way home from school. And they talked about it at dinner time and all evening long, until they went to sleep.

Mahmood was especially excited about the Dragon ride. When he had gone to Fun World before with his family, he was too small to ride it, but this year was different. This year, his father said that he could ride the Dragon Ride. It was so exciting – all the boys and girls in his class wanted to ride it, but none of them ever had. Mahmood was going to be the first one in his class to go on the Dragon Ride. He could hardly wait.

Every night at dinner, Mahmood and Zainab thanked their mother and father for planning this wonderful trip to Fun World.

Every night after dinner – Mahmood and Zainab cleared off the table. Then it was playtime. They played together, until it was time to go to bed.

"Mahmood, Zainab," their mother called on Monday night. "It's time to get ready for bed."

"Okay Mom," Zainab said and she went upstairs to get ready.

Mahmood was right in the middle of his puzzle. "I'll just finish this puzzle Mom," he said.

"Mahmood," his mother called, "you can finish your puzzle tomorrow. Now please go get ready for bed."

Mahmood looked at his puzzle. He was almost done. He couldn't leave now. He worked on his puzzle as fast as he could, but it was a hard puzzle and he was close.

"Mahmood," his father said, coming into the living room. "Your mother asked you to get ready for bed 15 minutes ago. Why are you still working on your puzzle?"

"Well, I'm almost done," Mahmood explained, adding another piece to his puzzle.

"Come on, it's time for bed. Go get ready."

"But my puzzle –" Mahmood said.

"You can finish it tomorrow," His father said.

Mahmood kept working on his puzzle. "Just two more minutes? Please?"

"Okay," his father said.

After two minutes, his father pointed to the clock. Mahmood didn't want to go upstairs. He didn't want to go to sleep. He was still wide awake.

"Dad," Mahmood said, "Tell me about the Dragon Ride."

"Not now Mahmood. Now it's time to go to bed." His father hugged him and kissed him good night. "*Assalaamu alaikum* Mahmood," he said.

"*Wa'alaikum Assalaam* Dad," Mahmood answered.

Mahmood headed up the stairs. He walked by Zainab's room – she was already in bed and the lights were turned off. Mahmood didn't want to go to sleep.

Mahmood went to the bathroom, brushed his teeth, and changed into his pajamas. Then Mahmood looked at his bed. He didn't want to lie down. He wasn't tired. He wanted to play.

"Just for a few minutes," he said, as he sat on the floor and played with his cars and trucks.

"Zoom! Zoom! Crash! Bang!" Mahmood zipped his cars around his room. This was fun.

Mahmood's mom opened his door. "Mahmood, it is way past your bedtime," she said. "Now put your toys away and get in bed."

"Okay," Mahmood said, putting his trucks away.

"*Assalaamu alaikum* Mahmood," she said as she tucked him into bed and hugged him and kissed him good night.

"*Wa'alaikum assalaam* Mom," Mahmood said as he watched his mother walk out of the room.

Mahmood lay in bed. He didn't feel sleepy. First he turned on one side. Then he turned on his other side. He wanted to get out of bed. He wanted to play.

'I know,' he thought, 'I can just read until I get sleepy.' And so Mahmood took out his book and began reading. He read one page, then another, and then another, and then another. Then, finally he said his prayers and went to sleep.

The next morning, Mahmood heard the alarm clock when it rang at seven o'clock. He ran to turn it off right away, and then he went to wake up the rest of his family. First he woke up his mom. Then, while she woke Zainab up, he woke up his dad.

This was Mahmood's job and he did it every single morning.

Every day of the week, Mahmood's parents told him when it was time to get ready for bed. And every day Mahmood went from his puzzles to his toys to his books. Mahmood was never tired enough to go to sleep at night. He always wanted to play or read or talk when it was bedtime.

On Tuesday night, when Mahmood's mom called him to get ready for bed, Mahmood didn't feel tired. So he kept on building a big home out of blocks.

"Mahmood," his mother called for the second time, "come on and get ready for bed."

But Mahmood played just a little longer.

"Mahmood," his father warned, "it's past your bedtime."

But Mahmood played just a little longer.

When Mahmood finally did go upstairs, he still didn't feel sleepy – so he played with his trucks in his room.

"Mahmood," his father said from the hallway. "Put them away and go to bed."

When Mahmood finally put his trucks away, and got into bed, he still wasn't sleepy. So he stayed up reading, until finally he felt sleepy. Then he said his prayers and went to sleep.

On Wednesday night, when it was time to get ready for bed, the same thing happened. Mahmood played one game after another. He tried every way he could so that he could stay awake just a little longer.

"I'm not sleepy," he told his parents.

"You're not sleepy now," his mom said, "But you'll be tired in the morning Mahmood."

And it was true. Even though Mahmood was wide awake at night, the next morning, he was very tired. When he heard the alarm clock ring at seven o'clock, he woke up and rolled in bed.

"I'm too tired! It's too early," he said. But it was his job to wake up the entire family, so off he went. He was so tired that he couldn't run to the alarm clock, so he walked over slowly to wake up his mother and his father.

That night though, he wasn't tired at all. He was really excited. Tomorrow was the last day of school and his class was having a pizza party and watching a movie! He was drawing a picture of Fun World, when his mother called him to get ready for bed. Well, I'm sure that you know what happened then. First he just kept drawing. Then when his father told him it was time to go to bed, he drew some more. Then when he finally did go up to bed, he played with his trucks, and then with his cars, and then with his blocks. Then when his mother came in and tucked him into bed, he read and read and read. Then he finally said his prayers and went to sleep.

Well, the next morning he was so tired, that he barely heard the alarm clock when it rang at seven o'clock. When he finally heard it, he woke up, but he felt so sleepy and so tired, that he couldn't get out of bed. He lay in bed for a few minutes, before he finally got up and walked slowly to the alarm clock to turn it off.

"*Assalaamu alaikum* Mom," he said. "It's time to get up."

"*Wa'alaikum assalaam* Mahmood," she said sitting up. "What's the matter?"

"I'm tired. I wish it wasn't time to get up already."

"Well, if you sleep earlier, then you won't be so tired," his mom said, going to wake Zainab up.

Mahmood woke up his father and went to get ready for school. He was so tired that he almost fell asleep while he was changing his clothes. Then he almost fell asleep at the breakfast table. And on the bus ride to school, he almost fell asleep.

At school, Mahmood almost fell asleep during story time. Then he almost fell asleep playing snakes and ladders. Then it was finally the time that he had been waiting for: it was time to watch the movie.

His teacher passed out the pizza, Mahmood looked at his piece – it looked delicious!

"*Bismillah Ar-rahmaan Ar-rahim*," he said. Then he said his dua and took a big bite. "Mmmm, this is yummy."

His teacher turned on the movie, and the students became silent. His teacher turned off the lights. As Mahmood ate his pizza he felt his eyelids becoming heavier and heavier. Soon, he pushed his pizza to the side of his desk and put his head down on his arms to watch the movie. But, before he knew what happened . . . Zzzzz. Zzzzz. Zzzzz. Zzzzz. Zzzzz. Zzzzz. Zzzzz. Zzzzz. Zzzzz. Zzzzz. Zzzzz. Zzzzz. Zzzzz. Zzzzz. Zzzzz. Mahmood was asleep. He slept right threw the movie!

"Mahmood, Mahmood, wake up,"

Mahmood suddenly sat up. Where was he? What was happening? Then he realized that he was at school – the movie. He looked over at the television, but it was turned off!

"What happened?" he asked, wide-eyed. "Aren't we going to watch the movie?"

"We already watched the movie Mahmood," his friends laughed. "You slept right through it!"

Mahmood shook his head. How awful it was for him to sleep through his class party. How terrible! He had wanted to watch the movie and chat with his friends.

"Can we still have some party time?" he asked.

"The party is over Mahmood," his teacher said. "It's time to go home."

By the time Mahmood got home, he was wide awake again because of the long nap he had taken at school. As they ate dinner, Zainab told their parents all about her last day of school.

"And then we played hot potato," she said. "And then we got to have free time and I played with my friends. And then we ate cupcakes and they were yummy!"

"*Masha'a* Allah," their father said. "Sounds like you had a terrific day!"

Zainab nodded happily.

"What about you, Mahmood?" his father asked.

"What did you do today?" his mother added.

"Um, uh, we – ahhh," Mahmood didn't really know what to tell his parents. He still couldn't believe that he had slept through the party.

"You had a pizza party, right?" his mother asked. "Was it nice?"

"Yeah," Mahmood said. "But I can't wait for Fun World tomorrow! That's what I'm really excited about!"

"Oh – me too!" cried Zainab, with a big grin on her face.

For the rest of dinner, Zainab and Mahmood chatted and chatted about Fun World! They asked their parents all kinds of questions and they became more and more excited.

At the end of dinner, they all said, "*Alhamdulillah.*"

Then Mahmood's father said, "Alright you two, now it's time to go to sleep. Don't forget that tomorrow we need to wake up at seven o'clock so that we can go to Fun World."

"Yes," their mother agreed, "it's very important that we wake up on time, because I heard that Fun World fills up very fast and when they have enough people, they don't let any more people in. We need to be there early so we can get in."

"Oh, I hope we make it," said Zainab, with a worried look on her face.

"Don't worry about it," Mahmood told them all. "Every morning, I hear the alarm clock and every morning, I wake you all up. It's my job. Tomorrow, I'll wake you up."

After Zainab and Mahmood helped clear the table, Zainab went upstairs to get ready for bed. But Mahmood didn't. He wasn't sleepy. He sat in the living room and played with his puzzles.

After a while, his father looked up and said, "Mahmood, it's time to go to sleep. You don't want to be tired at Fun World tomorrow."

So Mahmood went upstairs and changed into his pajamas and went to the bathroom and brushed his teeth. Then he said "Assalaamu alaikum" to his mom and dad and kissed them and hugged them goodnight. Then he went to his room. He lay down in his bed and tossed and turned and tossed and turned and tossed and turned.

Mahmood couldn't fall asleep, so he climbed out of bed and played with his cars quietly. He played and he played and he played. After a while, Mahmood got bored of playing with his cars, so he climbed back into bed.

But he still didn't want to sleep, so he took out his book and read and read and read. Before he knew it, he had finished his entire book. Well,

Mahmood still didn't want to go to sleep so he took out another book, and he read and read and read until he finished that book too!

Well, Mahmood still didn't want to got to sleep so he took out a third book and he read and read and read until his eyes began to close. He looked over at the watch. It was already past midnight. Mahmood closed his eyes, whispered his prayers, and drifted off into sleep.

All night long, Mahmood dreamt about the Dragon Ride and how he would ride it again and again and again. It was going to be so much fun.

But at seven o'clock when the alarm clock rang, nobody heard it and nobody woke up. Mahmood was so sleepy and tired from staying up so late that he slept right through it.

RING RING!

RING RING!

But nobody heard it.

RING RING!

RING RING!

But nobody woke up.

RING RING!

RING RING!

RING RING!

RING RING!

The alarm clock rang and rang and rang. Then because it had rang so much, it stopped ringing. When Mahmood finally woke up, he was surprised not to hear the alarm clock ringing.

"What's going on?" he thought, as he jumped out of bed and ran to the alarm clock.

"OH NO!" Mahmood exclaimed. "It's nine o'clock! We're so late! We're so late!"

Mahmood couldn't believe that they were so late! He ran to wake up his mother and father! They ran to wake up his sister! And everybody got ready as quickly as they could! Maybe they could still get to Fun World in time. The whole family got dressed and ate breakfast very very quickly! Then they rushed out to the car. Mahmood worried and worried the entire way to the park.

When they finally got there, he ran out of the car and into the line up. They waited in line for fifteen minutes and Mahmood worried and worried. He really wanted to ride the Dragon Ride. Finally when it was their turn, Mahmood's father said, "We would like two adult tickets and two children's tickets."

"I'm sorry Sir," the man replied, "but Fun World is all full. We can't let anyone else in."

"But please!" said Mahmood. "I want to ride the Dragon Ride! Please! Please!"

"I'm sorry," the man responded. "It's all full."

"Just us!" Mahmood said. "PLEASE!!! I need to go on the Dragon Ride!"

"Sorry," the man answered again, taking out a big sign and putting it right at the Fun World Gates. Mahmood read the sign – it said "Fun World – CLOSED"

"Come on Mahmood. It's time to go home," his mother said.

Mahmood couldn't believe it! He wanted to ride the Dragon Ride more than anything in the world and now he couldn't – just because he had stayed up late and so he couldn't wake up in the morning. As his father drove away, Mahmood put his face up against the window, reading the sign again: Fun World – CLOSED. Mahmood cried all the way home.

*****

SUGGESTED AGE GROUP
3 – 7 years old

BEHAVIORS ADDRESSED
• Not going to sleep at bedtime

BEHAVIORS MODELED

For Children
- To help their parents with house chores
- To say Bismillah before they eat
- To use Islamic phrases regularly, e.g., *Assalaamu alaikum, Masha'a Allah, Jazaakum Allahu khairan,* etc.

For Parents
- Stay calm when your children are not listening; however, Mahmood's parents needed to be more assertive in following through on the rules they set

CONCEPTS PRESENTED
- There are consequences for your actions, so if you make a bad choice, you will get bad results

IMPORTANT NOTE

A Must Do

When you are telling the story to your children, make sure to pause and comment about the character's bad behaviors while they are happening. Say things like "This is very wrong.", "How could they do such a thing?", "Oh, that's very bad." You can also ask the children if the characters are being "good boys/ bad boys." Although the story will show and explain this by the end, I strongly recommend that you don't wait until the end to point out which behaviors are wrong. This way, your child will not associate the bad behaviors with being fun and glamorous.

A Job Well Done

O nce upon a time, there were five animal friends who lived out in the wild. They were Bird, Chicken, Horse, Rabbit, and Donkey.

One day, when Chicken and Horse were standing together, Bird flew over.

"*Assalaamu alaikum*, Bird," said Chicken.

"Ooh, *wa'alaikum assalaam*," said Bird sounding worried.

"What's wrong Bird?" asked Horse.

"Oh, what will I do?" Bird asked them. "I'm so hungry. I have searched and searched and searched and I can't find any food to eat!"

Horse nodded. "I have the same problem!"

"Me too," said Chicken.

Just then, Rabbit hopped up to them. "*Assalaamu alaikum*," she said.

"*Wa'alaikum assalaam* Rabbit," they answered.

"Why are you all so sad?" she asked.

"Because we're hungry," Bird answered. "And we can't find any food to eat."

"You too?" asked Rabbit. "I was just talking to Donkey about how hungry we both are. We were going to ask you if you could share some of your food with us."

"We have no food to share," said Chicken.

The four animals were quiet and sad. What would they do?

There was no rain and so the grass and the plants weren't growing. Then Donkey came running up to them.

"What? What's the matter?" he asked. "Won't you share your food with us?"

"They have no food," answered Rabbit.

"Oh no!" cried Donkey. "What will we do?"

And the five animals were quiet and sad. What could they do? How would they find food?

"We have to find food," said Bird. "But how?"

The five animals thought and thought and thought.

"Oh Allah," said Rabbit, "please help us think of a way to find food."

And then they thought and thought and thought some more.

"Oh – I have an idea," Horse said. "We can plant our own food!"

"And grow it," said Chicken.

"And eat it," said Bird.

"But not so quickly," warned Horse. "This will take a long time and lots and lots of hard work from all of us."

"How long?" asked Rabbit. "Because I'm very hungry!"

"Very long," said Horse.

"An hour?" asked Bird.

"No," answered Horse.

"A day?" asked Donkey, licking his lips.

"No," answered Horse.

"Well then how long?" asked Chicken.

"It will probably take a month," said Horse.

Rabbit's eyes widened. Bird lowered his head. Donkey flicked his tail. And Chicken started clucking around in circles.

"Cluck cluck! Cluck cluck! That's too long! We'll starve before we eat!" Chicken yelled.

Bird started flying around the tree, going from one branch to the other. "Oh I'm so hungry! I'm so hungry!" he cried.

Donkey shook his head, "There has to be a faster way!" he said.

"There is no faster way," Rabbit scolded. "We'll keep searching and eat what we find, just like we do now, until our plants grow. Now you three need to calm down. You're wasting precious time! Let's get to work!"

"Okay," Horse said. "But it's going to be a lot of work. If we all work together, it will be easier. And then we can all eat the food together. Now, who wants to be part of the planting group?"

"I will," said Rabbit.

"Oh, me too!" said Chicken.

"Count me in," said Donkey.

"And me," cried Bird.

And so the five friends got to work, and a lot of work it was!

"First we have to find the seeds," said Horse.

"Oh, I can find seeds," said Bird. "Allah made me very good at finding seeds."

And so Bird flew off to look for seeds. He flew around and around and around. Then he landed on the ground and pecked and pecked and pecked at the dirt in the ground. When he found a seed he put it in his beak and flew back to his friends. Bird did this again and again. By the middle of the day, Bird had brought his friends a pile of seeds.

"Okay," Horse said. "Now we have to dig in the ground so that we can put the seeds in."

"Oh I can dig," said Rabbit. "Allah made me very good at digging."

"I can help too," said Horse.

And so Rabbit and Horse dug and dug and dug, until they had enough holes for all the seeds.

"Okay," Horse said. "Now, we need to put the seeds in the holes."

"Oh, I can do that," said Chicken. "Allah gave me a beak that I can use to put the seeds in the holes."

And so Chicken put one seed in the hole and then another and then another, until she was finished putting all the seeds in the ground.

"Okay," said Horse. "Now we need to put all the dirt back on top of the seeds to fill up the holes again."

"I can fill up the holes," said Donkey. "Allah gave me big hooves that will help me do it quickly."

And so Donkey used his hooves to fill up the holes and even out the ground until all the holes were filled.

Now, the sun was setting and it was getting dark.

"*Masha'a* Allah," exclaimed Rabbit, "it's already *Maghrib* time."

"We all did a lot of work today," added Donkey.

"*Alhamdulillah*," said Chicken.

"I'm exhausted," said Bird.

"Is there anything left to do?" asked Chicken. All the animals were tired. They wanted to go home and go to sleep.

"Well," said Horse, "there is one thing, but we've already worked so hard today. *Alhamdulillah*, we finished a lot of work. So let's go to sleep and we can work some more tomorrow."

And so all the animals went home and said their prayers in their own way[20] and went to sleep.

The next day, they all met around their planting spot.

"*Assalaamu alaikum* everybody," said Bird as he flew over.

"*Wa'alaikum assalaam* Bird," said his friends.

"You'll never believe what we're doing today," said Chicken.

"What?" asked Bird.

"We're digging a well," said Rabbit.

"Digging a well? Why? I thought we were just growing plants to eat," said Bird.

"Well, to grow plants, we need to water the seeds. And to water the seeds, we need water. And to get water we need a well," explained Rabbit.

"Horse and Donkey are looking for the perfect spot right now," said Chicken.

"We found the perfect spot," said Donkey running up to the other animals. "Horse is still over there. We all need to go back and help her. Let's go!"

---

20. The child may wonder if animals speak and say prayers like we do. A suggested answer could be, "Animals don't say their prayers the way we say it, because they don't speak human languages, but they still remember Allah and are grateful to Him."

In the Qur'an, ch. 17, v. 44, Allah says: "The seven heavens declare His glory and the earth (too), and those who are in them; and there is not a single thing but glorifies Him with His praise, but you do not understand their glorification; surely He is Forbearing, Forgiving"

And so they all went to dig the well with Horse. It was a hard job, and some animals could do more than others, but they all did their very best.

The animals dug and dug and dug until it was *Thuhr* time. "I'm tired," said Rabbit.

"Where's the water?" asked Bird.

"We've worked so hard," said Donkey.

"Let's take a break," suggested Chicken.

"Alright," said Horse.

And so they rested for a while, but not for very long. Soon, they were up and digging again. They dug and dug and dug until it was *Asr* time. But there was still no water.

They dug and dug and dug until it was *Maghrib* time and still, no water.

"Oh, it's getting dark," said Rabbit. "We had better go home now."

All the animals were so tired from the day's work, that they could hardly move. They slowly made their way home and said their prayers in their own way and went to sleep.

The next day they met around the digging spot, and they dug and dug and dug, until *Thuhr* time, but there was still no water.

Chicken said, "Will we ever be able to dig a well?"

"I don't think so. Water is very deep down in the ground," said Donkey.

Bird flew around the animals' heads and said, "Oh no! Oh no! Our seeds will die if we don't get water for them!"

"We have to dig a well, because how else can we get water?" asked Horse.

All of a sudden Bird, who was still flying around in circles, landed on Donkey's head, "I know! I think I know a place where we can get water!"

"Where? Where?" they all asked.

"There's this one place deep in the forest that I always fly over. I see water on the ground, but I can never reach it, because it's covered with dead branches."

"Deep in the forest?" asked Chicken, "I can't walk very far."

"Covered with dead branches?" asked Horse. "Those will be hard to move."

"No," said Bird. "Don't be so glum. Don't talk like that!"

"Yeah, we have to try," said Rabbit. "If we try our best then Allah will make it work for us."

"Rabbit is right," said Donkey. "Let's go look."

"Come on, I'll take you to the spot," Bird announced.

Chicken really couldn't walk that far, but the animals weren't going to leave her behind. Donkey sat down on the ground so that Chicken could climb up onto his back. And then he stood back up and all the animals headed into the forest. Bird took them exactly to the spot.

There the animals worked hard moving the dead branches away, hoping that there was a lot of water underneath. When *Maghrib* time came, the animals still hadn't moved all the branches, and they still hadn't found the water. It was getting dark and they were tired, so the animals went home and said their prayers and went to sleep.

The next day, the animals met early at their planting spot and again they all went back into the forest together. They worked hard, moving branch after branch until finally, by *Thuhr* time they had moved all the branches. And there it was – an abandoned well!

"We've got water! We've got water!" sang Bird, overjoyed as he flew around.

"*Alhamdulillah! Alhamdulillah!*" said Chicken, jumping up and down.

All the animals jumped up and down and thanked Allah. They had worked so hard to find the water and Allah had helped them so much. There was just one problem.

"How will we get the water out of the well?" asked Rabbit.

"Oh no," cried Bird. "After all this work, and now we have no way of getting the water out of the well!"

Chicken looked glum. Horse hung her head. But Donkey looked happy, "Remember," he said to his friends. "Allah will help us if we try our best. Now don't look so sad – get up and look around. Maybe we will find something that can help us."

"Donkey's right," Horse said. "Allah will help us if we try. Come on – let's look around."

And so all the animals searched and searched, but by *Asr* time, they still hadn't found anything. Well, they searched some more and just before *Maghrib* time, Horse came running over to his friends with a bucket!

"Look!" he exclaimed. "Look what I found! A bucket! And it has a rope tied to it too!"

"The people that used to use this well must have left it behind," said Bird.

"*Alhamdulillah! Alhamdulillah!*" all the animals cried. They were so happy. But, now it was *Maghrib* time and the sun was setting so it was time for the animals to go home.

The next day, the animals met around the planting spot and went into the forest. Today, they had to fetch the water from the well and water the plants. It was hard work, but together, they filled up the bucket and pulled it out of the well. They carried the bucket all the way back to the planting spot. There, they watered the seeds.

"We need more water," said Rabbit.

And so they went back into the forest. Together, they lowered the bucket into the well and filled it up with water. Then they pulled the heavy bucket back up with all their might. And they took turns, two by two carrying the heavy bucket on the long walk back to the planting spot.

After they watered all the plants, they were all tired out from the day's work and they wanted to go to sleep.

There was just one problem.

"If we leave the planting spot and go to sleep," Horse said, "someone could take our food during the night."

"But we still don't have any food," said Rabbit. "It's just some seeds in the ground."

"Birds could eat the seeds," said Bird.

"So could chickens," said Chicken.

"Then we have to have a guard," said Horse.

"Oh, that's a good idea," said Donkey.

"Someone to stay up all night and watch and guard and make sure that nobody takes the food," explained Horse.

"I can guard tonight," said Chicken.

And so it was decided. All the other animals went home and Chicken stayed up all night and guarded the seeds.

The next day, the animals fetched some water from the well and watered their plants. Then that night, Donkey stayed up all night to guard the seeds. And the next day, the animals fetched water from the well and watered their plants.

Day after day, they watered their plants. Night after night, they guarded their plants. Waiting and hoping and praying to Allah that the plants would grow and that they would all have enough to eat. All the animals worked hard at watering the plants and they all took turns staying up at night to guard. First Chicken, then Donkey, then Rabbit, then Horse, then Bird, then Chicken again. And so on and so forth.

Until one morning, after Rabbit had been guarding for the night, the animals saw the plants! Finally after all their watering and guarding, the seeds had grown into plants and they were coming out of the ground!

"Oh *Alhamdulillah!*" exclaimed Bird, happy to see them.

"We're going to have a yummy, yummy breakfast" added Rabbit, running toward the plants.

"*Bismillah*," said Donkey.

"Not so fast," said Chicken. "The plants are still very small. If we eat them now, there won't even be enough for today. There won't be enough for us all to eat."

"Chicken's right," agreed Horse. "We have to wait for the plants to grow taller. That way, when we eat some, we'll still have more. And then there will be enough for all of us."

"Oh, they're right," Rabbit said.

"But I'm so hungry," said Bird.

"Me too," added Donkey.

"We'll just have to find some other food for breakfast," said Chicken. "We need to leave these plants grow bigger."

"I think we need to put a guard on all the time now," said Rabbit. "Day and night. With the beautiful green plants sticking out of the ground, we definitely have to guard them!"

"She's right," said Horse. "I'll guard today." And so the other animals went to look for breakfast and to get water for the plants while Horse guarded all day long. Then at night Bird guarded, then Chicken, then Donkey, then Rabbit, then Horse again.

So every day, the animals watered the plants. And all day and all night one of the animals guarded the plants. The plants grew and grew and grew, but they still weren't big enough to feed everybody. The animals were hungry and they looked at the plants. They wanted to eat them.

One morning, Chicken announced, "Okay! That's enough waiting. The plants have grown tall and I am too hungry to wait anymore. Let's eat!"

"No, we can't do that," said Rabbit. "The plants are not very tall at all Chicken."

"We're all hungry," said Horse, "but if we eat them now, then there won't be enough for all of us. We have to wait."

"Oh, but I can't wait any longer," said Bird.

"Me neither," added Donkey. "I think it's time to eat them."

"If we eat them now," Horse said, "then this is how little each of us will get to eat." Horse pointed with her nose at the little, eensy weensy bit that each animal would eat.

"Oh no no no," said Donkey. "That won't be enough."

"Oh then we'll have to wait," agreed Chicken.

"But I'm just too hungry to wait," Bird said.

"You'll just have to find something else to eat Bird," said Rabbit. "We need to let the plants grow taller, so that there will be enough for us to eat."

All the animals nodded and they walked away, hungry, leaving Chicken to guard the plants for the day.

Chicken guarded the plants all day long, while the other animals fetched water from the well and watered them. When *Maghrib* time came, Donkey walked over to Chicken.

"*Assalaamu alaikum* Chicken," he said.

"*Wa'alaikum assalaam* Donkey," Chicken answered.

"I'm here to guard for the night," Donkey said.

"Oh good," she answered, "because I was getting sleepy." Chicken went home to sleep for the night and left Donkey all alone, guarding the plants so nobody would eat them.

The sun set and the moon rose and Donkey sat and looked at the plants. In the moonlight, the plant looked tall enough to eat and Donkey watched it dreamily.

"What's the matter with them?" Donkey said. "These are big tall plants. There's enough to eat and make me very full. They're wrong about waiting. We planted these plants so we could eat, not so we could stay hungry!"

Donkey licked his lips and looked at the plants. They looked delicious. He was so hungry. Why did he have to wait? Why?

"This doesn't make any sense," Donkey said. His stomach growled. "I'm sitting here, right in front of these beautiful, delicious plants and I'm hungry, hungry, hungry! No, the rest of the animals are wrong. I worked hard to plant these plants and every day, I work very hard to bring them water and to guard them. I deserve to eat them. I shouldn't be hungry!"

In the dark, dark night, Donkey stood up, and he walked over to the plants. He looked all around him to make sure that nobody was there. He didn't see anybody. Donkey began to eat.

Munch, munch, munch, he chewed. The plants were delicious! Donkey ate faster and faster and more and more, until finally he was full.

"Oh," Donkey said as he sat back down, his belly heavy. "It feels so good to be full." And for the rest of the night, Donkey stared at the moon and patted his full stomach. But when Fajr time came and the sun began to rise and it was light out, Donkey got worried. He had eaten all the plants! There was nothing left! What would he tell the other animals? They would be so angry with him.

When the other animals came, they were shocked and sad and mad and hungry!

"Where are our plants?" asked Bird

"How could someone eat them?" asked Rabbit.

"Weren't you guarding, Donkey?" asked Chicken.

"Who ate them?" asked Horse.

Donkey looked from Bird to Rabbit to Chicken to Horse. They looked really, really mad! If he told them, they would hate him – they would never talk to him again!

"I don't know what happened," Donkey lied.

"How can you not know? You were the one guarding last night," said Chicken.

"Yes, but – but – but ," Donkey thought hard. What could he say? How could he save himself? Then he had an idea. "This is what happened," he said. "Last night when I was guarding, it got very dark and I got very, very sleepy. Then, without meaning to, I fell asleep. And when I woke up, the plants were all eaten – just like that. So somebody must have eaten them while I was sleeping," Donkey lied again.

"Somebody ate them! Somebody ate our plants!" screamed Bird, flying around.

"Did you eat them Bird?" asked Horse. "Yesterday, you said that you were too hungry to wait!"

"No! I didn't eat them!" answered Bird. "Did you eat them, Horse?"

"No! What about you Chicken? Did you eat them?" Horse asked.

"I didn't eat them!" Chicken said. "I went home and slept all night long! Did you eat them Rabbit?"

"No! I didn't eat them," said Rabbit sadly. "Did you eat them Donkey?"

"No!" Donkey lied. "I didn't eat them. I guarded them until I fell asleep."

"Somebody is lying!" yelled Bird.

"We'll never know who it is," said Chicken, "because Donkey was asleep and nobody else was there!"

"That's not true," said Rabbit. "Somebody else was there."

"Who? Who was there? Were you there?" asked Horse. "Do you know who did it?"

"No," said Rabbit. "I wasn't there, and I don't know who did it. But Allah was there and Allah knows who did it."

"That's true," said Chicken. "But how will we figure out who ate the plants?"

"I have an idea to figure it out," said Horse.

The animals all gathered around Horse to hear her plan.

"All of us need to go down to the well," Horse explained. "And every one of us will take a turn jumping over the well. Before we jump, we will make a *dua* to Allah. We will ask Him to make us fall into the well if we are telling a lie. So, after that *j77*

, we will see. If you can jump over the well, then you didn't eat the plants. But if you fall in, then you ate the plants and you're lying about it."

"Yes! Yes!" the animals agreed.

"But that's not fair," said Chicken, looking worried. "Rabbit and Horse are good at jumping. And Donkey is very big. But Bird and I, we don't know how to jump very far and we're small. We won't make it over the well."

"Don't worry," said Rabbit. "If you're telling the truth, then Allah will make you jump over the well. You'll only fall in if you're lying."

And so all the animals went down to the well. There, they stood in a line and got ready to find out who was lying.

First, it was Horse's turn. She walked up to the well and she said,
"Oh Allah, Oh Allah,
Who ate the food, only You saw.

If I ate the food and did not tell
Then make me fall into the well."

And then, Horse jumped over the well and she landed safely on the other side.

"*Alhamdulillah*," Horse exclaimed.

"So then, Horse didn't do it," said Chicken.

"It's your turn Bird," said Horse. "Go ahead."

"But I'm so scared," said Bird. "I have such small small legs and the well is very, very big. Can I fly over?"

"No," Rabbit answered. "You have to jump."

"Then I'll fall in!" Bird cried. "I'm just not big enough to jump over the well."

"Are you telling the truth?" asked Rabbit. "Or did you eat the plants?"

"No! I didn't eat the plants," answered Bird. "I am telling the truth."

"Then it doesn't matter how small you are," Rabbit explained. "Allah will help you!"

"Oh, I'm really, really scared!" Bird said. He was shaking with fear. His small legs were shaking. His wings were shaking. His head was shaking. Even his little beak was shaking.

"If you're telling the truth bird," said Chicken. "Then Allah will give you the power to jump."

Bird stepped up to the well. He was still shaking with fear. In a tiny, scared voice, he said:

"Oh Allah, Oh Allah,
Who ate the food, only You saw.
If I ate the food and did not tell
Then make me fall into the well."

Then Bird closed his eyes tightly, because he was so afraid. Then, he jumped as hard as he could and somehow, somehow, . . . he landed safely on the other side of the well.

"*Masha'a* Allah! *Masha'a* Allah!" exclaimed Horse.

"You're safe because you told the truth!" Rabbit said.

"I've never seen a little bird jump so far!" said Chicken.

"See how Allah helps you if you tell the truth," said Horse.

Donkey began to sweat. What would he do? How could he save himself now?

"It's your turn, Rabbit," said Horse.

Rabbit stepped up to the well. She took a deep, deep breath and said, "Oh Allah, Oh Allah,

Who ate the food, only You saw.

If I ate the food and did not tell

Then make me fall into the well."

Then Rabbit jumped as hard as she could over the well. And she landed safely on the other side.

"*Alhamdulillah*," said Rabbit as she landed.

"*Masha'a* Allah," exclaimed Bird.

"Your turn, Chicken," said Horse.

Chicken clucked and clucked and walked around in circles, pecking at the ground. "How will I do it? How will I do it?" she asked.

"Come on Chicken," said Bird. "You have nothing to worry about if you're telling the truth."

"I'll fall in! I'll fall in," Chicken worried. She walked and pecked and pecked and walked and worried. "I'm not big enough. Sure – it was easy for Rabbit. Rabbit is always jumping. I've never jumped before in my life! I'll fall into the well."

"Chicken," Rabbit said, "just like you told Bird, it's not about how well you can jump. Are you telling us the truth?"

"Yes," Chicken answered. "Oh yes, I am telling the truth."

"Then Allah will help you. Allah always helps those who tell the truth."

"Come on Chicken," said Horse. But Chicken was too afraid to do it. So Horse and Bird came around the well and tried to make Chicken step upto to the well. Horse pushed her from her tail and Bird pulled her from her wing, until finally, Chicken was standing at the edge of the well.

"Ah! I'm going to fall," she screamed.

"Say the *dua*, Chicken, and if you're telling the truth, then Allah will keep you safe," said Rabbit.

Well Chicken stood at the edge of the well, scared as can be, and she said the *dua*.

"Oh Allah, Oh Allah,

Who ate the food, only You saw.

If I ate the food and did not tell

Then make me fall into the well."

Then, with a terribly frightened scream, Chicken jumped as far as she could. But you have to remember that Chicken had never jumped before in her life and that, by herself, she just couldn't jump that far.

But somehow, somehow, Chicken jumped right over the well and landed safely on the other side.

"*Masha'a* Allah!" said Horse.

"So you were telling the truth," said Rabbit.

"See," said Bird, "see how Allah helps those who tell the truth."

"*Alhamdulillah*," said Chicken with a great big sigh of relief. She was so happy to be safe and sound on the other side of the well. "Allah really did help me because I told the truth."

"Your turn, Donkey," said Horse.

"Well, I uhhh, ummm, uhh, I'm a little tired right now. Maybe I could take a little nap and then try to jump after the nap," Donkey said.

"Oh Donkey," said Rabbit, "you're afraid. But if you're telling the truth, you have nothing to be scared about. Just say the *dua* and Allah will help you."

"Yeah Donkey," said Chicken. "If Bird and I could do it, then you can definitely do it. You are so much bigger."

But the problem was that Donkey wasn't telling the truth and so he had a lot to be scared about.

"Oh, I don't know. I don't feel very well. I really think I should just rest a while and then jump afterward," said Donkey.

"No Donkey," said Horse. "It's your turn and you need to jump now."

Donkey looked at Horse. He looked at Rabbit and Chicken and Bird. They were all looking at him, waiting for him to jump. And so Donkey stepped up to the well and he said the *dua*.

"Oh Allah, Oh Allah,

Who ate the food, only You saw.

If I ate the food and did not tell

Then make me fall into the well."

And then he took a deep breath and jumped as hard as he could. Now Donkey had strong, long legs, and he was very big, but he was not telling the truth. And so, halfway through his jump, Donkey fell into the well.

"Donkey," Rabbit yelled, running up to the well.

"He's the one who ate the food then," said Bird.

The animals gathered around the well and looked down. There was Donkey, in the water.

"Help! Help!" he called. "Help me - I 'm sinking!"

"You ate the food," yelled Horse. "And you lied to us!"

"I'm really sorry!" Donkey yelled, "I'll never lie again. Please help me!"

"We trusted you! You were supposed to be guarding the plants," Chicken yelled, "and you ate them all!"

"You let us down!" screamed Bird.

"Please help! My legs are sinking in! Help me! I'm sorry!" said Donkey.

"How could you eat them all? We all worked so hard to plant them!" Rabbit yelled.

"Oh pleeeeeeeeeeeeeeeeeeeeeease! Pleeeeeeeeeeeeeease help!" Donkey yelled, "I'm sinking into the water. I'm going to die!"

"You deserve it!" Bird yelled. "You lied to us! And you betrayed us!"

"I'll never lie again! I'll never betray you again!" Donkey said.

"And why should we believe you?" yelled Rabbit. "You lied before – you're lying again now!"

"Yeah," agreed Horse, "you just want to save yourself. You don't care about us!"

"Pleeeeeeeeeeeease!" yelled Donkey. "My neck is sinking in! The water's going to reach my head – I won't be able to breathe."

"You deserve it!" said Horse. "You brought it to yourself!"

"We should just leave you here!" yelled Chicken.

"No! Please! Please! I learned my lesson! I'll never lie again! I – I (gurgle, gurgle)"

The water had reached Donkey's nose and he couldn't breathe anymore. He was sinking in the well.

Bird yelled, "Pull him out! Pull him out! We can't let him die!"

Chicken looked down at Donkey with her empty stomach – she was angry with him, but she didn't want him to die. "Maybe he really did learn his lesson," she said.

"He had better never lie to us again!" said Horse.

Rabbit ran to get the bucket and threw it into the well for Donkey. All the animals held the rope tightly as Donkey bit hard on the bucket. Together, the animals pulled and pulled and pulled as hard as they could. Donkey was heavy and it was hard work. Donkey did his best to climb up the sides. The animals pulled and Donkey climbed and the animals pulled and Donkey climbed, until finally he came out of the well.

"I'm sorry," Donkey said to them. "I'm sorry that I ate the plants. And I'm sorry that I lied to you. Now I know that lying is bad. Please forgive me. I'll never do it again."

"Okay – we'll forgive you, but we hope you've learned your lesson," they said.

"Oh, I've learned my lesson. I'll never tell another lie for as long as I live," said Donkey.

And he never did.

*****

SUGGESTED AGE GROUP
3 – 6 years old

Behaviors Addressed
• Lying

BEHAVIORS MODELED

For Children
• To pray to Allah when they need something
• Cooperation
• Hard Work
• To appreciate the abilities that Allah gave them and to use them for good
• To say their prayers before going to sleep
• To rethink their plan and change part of their plan to make it work when their plan doesn't work
• To go home before dark and stay out only when it's safe
• Patience
• Forgiveness
• To use Islamic phrases regularly, e.g., *Assalaamu alaikum, Masha'a* Allah, *Jazaakum Allahu khairan*, etc.

CONCEPTS PRESENTED
• Telling the truth is always the right thing to do
• Lying is wrong
• Working together makes everybody's job easier
• If you try your best, Allah will help you
• Allah sees and knows everything
• Allah helps those who are honest

Only at the Park

Once upon a time, there was a little boy named Ahmed. Ahmed was five years old and he lived with his mom, his dad, his older brother Dawud and his baby sister Haleema. Ahmed's favourite time was summertime. He loved to play at the park with Dawud and throw a ball around with his entire family. Ahmed was a good boy and he always did his best to help his mom and dad and do his chores.

One summer morning, as Ahmed lay in his bed asleep, the sun's light snuck in through the curtains and landed on his face. Ahmed, stretched and turned and slowly opened his eyes and said his morning dua.

"Ashhadu an laa ilaaha illa Allah, wa ashhadu anna Muhammadan rasool Allah," [21] he said as he sat up in bed. Ahmed saw that Dawud's bed was empty and that he wasn't in the room. He must have already woken up. Ahmad wanted to find Dawud, but first, he had to finish his morning jobs. Ahmad made his bed as neatly as he could. Then he went out into the hallway. "Assalaamu alaikum!" he announced to his family.

"Wa'alaikum assalaam Ahmed," his mother and Dawud called back.

"Go brush your teeth Ahmed, and then come down to have your breakfast please," his mom told him. So, he went to brush his teeth. Ahmed was very good at brushing his teeth now that he was a big five-year old boy. He stood there, brushing and brushing, being careful not to miss a single spot. He looked in the mirror at his mouth. He watched the brush go over his teeth. He wanted to see it better, so he bit the brush between his teeth, and putting his two hands on the counter, he lifted his whole body up onto the counter. There he sat on his knees, right up

---

21. I bear witness that there is no God but Allah, and that Muhammad is the messenger of Allah.

against the mirror, brushing and brushing and brushing. Then he rinsed his mouth and opened wide to look at his clean teeth in the mirror.

"Ahmed!" his mother suddenly said from the doorway. "Get down right now! That's dangerous Ahmed, you shouldn't be up there."

"Okay Mom," Ahmed said as he came down from the countertop.

He followed his mother into the kitchen, where Dawud was already sitting at the table, playing with his cars.

"*Assalaamu alaikum Ahmed*," Dawud said.

"*Wa' alaikum asalaam*," Ahmed answered.

Ahmed came over to sit next to Dawud. "Let me play," he said. And, because Dawud was a good boy, he gave Ahmed one of the cars and they played together.

"Alright boys," said their mother, "breakfast is almost ready. Can you please set three plates and three forks on the table."

The two boys jumped up.

"I'll get the plates," announced Dawud.

"Then I'll get the forks," announced Ahmed. And they quickly got the plates and forks and set them on the table.

"*Masha'a* Allah," said their mom, "what wonderful little helpers I have."

And just as their mother turned around from the stove, she saw something *awful*. "Ahmed!" she yelled in horror. "Get down from there this instant."

Ahmed had climbed up onto his chair and from there he had climbed up onto the edge of the table. He stood there on top of the table looking down at the ground, looking down to see how high up he was.

"Okay Mom," Ahmed said. "I'm coming down!" and he got ready to jump.

"No! No!" his mother said, but it was too late. Ahmed had already jumped into the air and landed down on the ground. "Ahmed!" his mother yelled angrily. "I just told you this morning, that is very, very, very dangerous. No jumping in the house."

"But you told me to get down Mom," he said. "I was just getting down."

"You didn't need to jump to get back down, you could have climbed back down onto your chair. But you shouldn't have been up there in the first place Ahmed. No climbing on furniture."

"Oh, but Mom," Ahmed protested. "I'm very good at climbing."

"I know you are Ahmed, but it's too dangerous here. No climbing in the house. You can climb at the park. You can climb the trees. You can climb the play structure. But you can't climb in the house. Do you understand?" she asked.

"Yeah," Ahmed nodded.

"Now, sit down and let's have our breakfast," she said.

Ahmed sat down on his chair and, together with Dawud read the dua: "*Alahuma baarik lanaa feemaa razaktana wa qinaa 'athaaba annaar*[22]. *Bismillah*" And using their right hands, they began eating their scrambled eggs.

"Oh, *Jazaaki Allahu khairan*," said Dawud to his mom.

"Yeah," Ahmed agreed, "this is yummy!"

"*Alhamdulillah* – I'm glad you like it," their mother answered, smiling.

"What are we doing today, Mom?" asked Dawud as he munched away.

"Can we go out?" asked Ahmed.

"Actually," their mother smiled, "you boys are very lucky. Remember how you've been wanting to go out with your friends, Ameen and Mohamed?"

"Yes!" they nodded excitedly.

"Well, yesterday, I spoke with their mother and today, we can all meet at the park so you can play together."

---

22. Oh Allah bless what you have given us, and protect us from the hell fire. In the name of Allah.

"Oh – yes yes yes yes yes!" said Ahmed, pumping his fist in the air. "*Alhamdulillah*! *Alhamdulillah*!"

"Woo! Hoo! *Alhamdulillah*!" Dawud joined in the cheering.

"When are we going?" asked Ahmed.

"As soon as we finish breakfast, we can start getting ready," their mother said. "I'll need your help. While I feed Haleema and get her dressed and get myself ready, you two will need to clear the table, wash your hands, and dress yourselves. Then I need you to wash the fruit and put it in a bag so that we can take it to the park with us for a snack. Then we can leave. Can you do that boys?"

"Oh yes we can!" they answered together. Ahmed and Dawud were used to helping their mom get things ready. It made things easier for everybody. And it helped them go out to the park a lot faster!

So when Ahmed and Dawud finished their breakfast they said "*Alhamdulillah*."

"You can go upstairs to get Haleema ready," said Dawud.

"Yeah, we'll do the work down here," Ahmed said.

And so their mother went upstairs and the boys got to work. First, they carefully cleared the table, taking all the dishes and the forks to the sink. Then they took a wet washcloth and they wiped the tabled clean, taking all of the crumbs off.

"Look, it's shining!" said Ahmed.

"Great. Looks like we're done in the kitchen," said Dawud. The boys went into the bathroom and washed their hands. Then they went to their room and looked on their beds. There, their mother had put down two different outfits. It was their job to choose which outfit they wanted to wear and it was their job to put the other one away.

Ahmed chose his green T-shirt and his orange pants and he put them on. Then it was time to put away his other outfit and his pajamas. Ahmed took the clothes and put them into the closet. Standing there at the closet, he looked up and saw the bar hanging in the closet. "Hey, it's like the monkey bars," he said, jumping up, trying to reach it. He jumped once, twice, three times and finally he was able to hold on to the bar.

"Look! Look Dawud!" Ahmed said, "Look at me, I'm hanging in the closet like the clothes!" Ahmed laughed and swung back and forth.

"Get down!" Dawud said. "Mom told you not to."

"But look," Ahmed said, "it's so fun!" Ahmed swung his body a little back and forth, then a little more, back and forth, then even more, back and forth and –

"OUCH!" he said, letting go and falling to the ground. "Ow, my leg!"

"What happened?" asked Dawud.

"It hit the wall in the closet," said Ahmed. "It hurts."

"Well I told you not to do that," Dawud said. "Next time you should listen." Dawud helped Ahmed get up and walk over to his bed. "You rest here until your knee gets better. I'll go down and wash the fruit."

"Oh, but I want to wash the fruit," whined Ahmed.

"Too bad, you should have listened," said Dawud. "Remember to say your *dua* to ask Allah to make it feel better Ahmed. That way you'll feel better soon." And Dawud walked out of the room.

Ahmed lay on his bed and made dua for Allah to make his leg feel better. "*Allahuma ishfinee bishifaa' ak, wa daawiny bidawaa' ak.*"[23]

"Ahmed! Dawud!" their mother called after a little while. "I'm ready. Are you all finished with the fruit?"

"Yes Mom," called Dawud, "I'll be right up."

Ahmed stood up. His leg was feeling better – Allah had healed it! He went over to his mom and she helped him tie his shoelaces and then they were off to the park!

At the park, Ahmed and Dawud ran up to Ameen and Mohamed. Ahmed was so happy to see them. Together, they climbed on the play structure and swung on the bars. They climbed the trees and swung from the branches. They climbed and they jumped and they played. And Ahmed really was a very good jumper.

"Mom look at me!" he called as he jumped down from the bar.

---

23. Oh Allah cure me with your cure, and make me recover with your medicine.

Clap! Clap! Clap! His mother clapped for him and smiled. Ahmed loved the park. He loved playing with his friends. He had a terrific time.

When he had climbed and jumped and swung and ran to his heart's content and he was all tired out, Ahmed said Assalaamu alaikum to his friends and rode back home with his family.

"See what a good climber I am Mom?" asked Ahmed.

"You are a terrific climber Ahmed," his mother said. "And a wonderful jumper, and a very good runner. And I'm happy to see you had so much fun. I like it when you climb and run and jump in the park Ahmed. Just remember not to do it at home, because it's dangerous."

"Okay," Ahmed agreed. "I won't."

They were all very tired from their wonderful time at the park. Ahmed's baby sister Haleema fell asleep in the car. When they got home, Ahmed and Dawud ate lunch and then went into their room to take a nap.

"Have a good nap, my little climbers," their mother said as she put them to bed. "You spent a lot of energy. *Assalamu alaikum.*"

And with that the two boys fell off into sleep. When they woke up from their nap, their mother told them to go ahead and go out to the living room and play, but to keep their voices down.

"I'm trying to put Haleema to sleep, so I need you to be nice and quiet," she said.

Ahmed and Dawud nodded quietly and tip-toed out of the room and into the living room. There they took out their quiet games, their puzzles, their building blocks and Lego's and they played with them for a while.

Dawud was working on a puzzle, but it was very hard. Ahmed helped a little and then he got bored with it, so he turned to play with the blocks. He built a house and a bridge and then CRASH! They fell! Haleema's cry came from the next room.

"Oh no," Ahmed said, "I think I woke her up!"

"You'd better not do that anymore," Dawud told him.

"But I didn't mean it, the blocks just fell," Ahmed explained.

"Well, maybe you shouldn't play with the blocks right now," Dawud said, "because they make a lot of noise when they fall."

"Well then what should I do?" Ahmed asked.

"I don't know," said Dawud, as he continued playing with his puzzle.

Ahmed sat on the couch and thought, but he was bored. Soon he stood up and began jumping on the couch – it was fun and it didn't make any noise! He jumped and jumped and jumped! Higher and higher and higher!

"Ahmed," said Dawud, "Mom said not to."

Ahmed knew Dawud was right, but it was just too much fun, so he kept on jumping. Then Ahmed got an idea, he could jump from the back of the couch onto the seats. So he climbed up onto the back of the couch and jumped onto the seat – what fun! So he did it again and again and again.

"Ahmed," said Dawud, "Mom said not to."

Ahmed knew Dawud was right, but it was just too much fun, so he kept on jumping. Then he saw the sides of the couch, the arm rests, so he climbed onto those and threw himself lying down onto the couch – what fun! So he climbed up on to the side and jumped and he did it again and again and again.

"Ahmed," said Dawud, "Mom said not to."

Ahmed knew Dawud was right, but it was just too much fun, so he kept on jumping.

"Ahmed!" screamed his mother from the doorway of the living room. "What are you doing?"

"Just playing," said Ahmed.

"Ahmed, these kinds of games are not for inside the house – it's too dangerous. You could hurt yourself. Now I don't want to see it again. Do you understand?"

"Yeah," said Ahmed. "But I won't hurt myself. I won't. I'm good at it."

"That doesn't matter Ahmed. It's dangerous and you can hurt yourself. Now, no more jumping or climbing in the house."

"*Assalaamu alaikum*," called their father from the doorway.

"Dad's home! Dad's home!" the two boys sang happily, running to see their father. "Wa'alaikum assalaam," they said, hugging him, one on either side.

"How are you boys?" he asked.

"Good, good, good," answered Ahmed.

"We went to the park today," said Dawud.

"And played with Mohamed and Ameen," added Ahmed.

"Well, sounds like you had quite the day," their father smiled as he walked into the living room. "Ah, I'm starving, but it looks to me like you boys have some cleaning up to do before we eat. So, I'll go wash up and you boys clean up and set the table, then I can hear all about your day at dinner. Do we have a deal?"

"We have a deal!" Ahmed and Dawud agreed.

And so the boys buzzed around the living room, cleaning up their toys quickly. Once they were finished, they went into the kitchen to help their mom with dinner.

"Okay boys," Mom said, "you can set the table. We need plates, and spoons, and forks, and napkins."

Ahmed took out two plates and put them in their spot on the table. Then he went back for the next two plates. Dawud was already putting out the spoons and forks, so Ahmed got the napkins from his mom and put one napkin next to each plate.

"There, all done," he said. "Mom! You can bring out the food – the table is all set!"

"In a minute *insha'a* Allah," Mom said.

Ahmed waited a minute, but Mom still didn't bring out the food. "Mom, aren't you going to bring out the food? The table is set," Ahmed told her.

"I'm just finishing the salad, Ahmed," Mom said.

So Ahmed went to call his Dad, but he was in the bathroom.

"Just wait at the table, Ahmed," Dad told him. "I'll be there in a minute."

Ahmed went to the table and sat down. Dawud was in the living room reading a book. Mom was in the kitchen, finishing the food, and Dad was in the bathroom washing up. Ahmed was all alone in the dining room. He looked around him at the table. He looked at the walls and then, he looked at the ceiling. There, right in the middle of the ceiling was the lamp, hanging down into the room. 'Neat,' Ahmed thought, 'I bet I can reach it.' And he stood up.

Ahmed climbed up onto the seat of his chair, but he couldn't reach it from there. So Ahmed climbed onto the table, careful not to step on any of the plates. He reached his hand up in the air as far as he could – and he *almost* touched the lamp. He stood on his tiptoes and stretched and stretched as far up as he could, and he almost reached the lamp. He jumped up to try to touch it. He jumped once, almost touched it, and then landed back on the table. He jumped up again and he touched it!

Then – CRASH!

When Ahmed came back down after the jump, one foot missed the table! He fell to the floor with a horrible BANG! As he was falling, he hit his chin on the table – SMACK! And then he landed on the floor. Now Ahmed was screaming and crying. There was blood squirting out of his chin! There was blood on the table, blood on the floor, blood on the chair, blood on his face, and blood on his shirt and his pants. He was bleeding hard.

His mother came running in from the kitchen. "Ahmed!" she exclaimed.

His father came running out from the bathroom, "Ahmed!" he exclaimed.

His brother came running in from the living room, "Oh no!" he yelled.

His mother rushed to his side and held him tight. Ahmed cried loudly. His chin hurt him so much!

"Owwwwww! Owwwwww! Owwwww!" he cried in pain.

His father ran into the bathroom and grabbed a clean cloth. His mother held the cloth against his chin. She tried to stop the bleeding, but it didn't stop. Soon the cloth was full of blood, and Ahmed was still crying in pain.

"Owwwwww! Owwwwww! Owwwwww!"

His father brought a second cloth. His mother held it against his chin and tried to stop the bleeding, but it didn't stop. Ahmed was still crying in pain.

"Owwwwww! Owwwwww! Owwwwww!"

"Oh no! Is he going to be okay?" asked Dawud.

"This is a very bad cut," Mom said. "I don't think we'll be able to take care of it here."

"I'll have to take him to the hospital," said Dad. He picked Ahmed up and carried him out to the car. Ahmed was still crying in pain: "Owwwwww! Owwwwww! Owwwwww!"

All the way to the hospital Ahmed cried and cried. He was still bleeding and his chin hurt him terribly. As he held the cloth to his chin, he felt his fingers start to get wet.

"Oh no!" he said. "The blood is coming through – my fingers are getting bloody. The blood's going to come all over me!"

"Here," his father said, handing him a clean cloth. "Hold this up to your chin instead. The other cloth has already filled up with blood."

Ahmed held the cloth to his chin. It hurt.

"Owwwwww! Owwwwww! Owwwwww!" Ahmed cried in pain. He cried and he cried until they finally reached the hospital.

At the hospital, the nurses looked at him and shook their heads – "Poor little boy," they said. "He's going to need stitches." They took him to a room and his father lay him down on the bed. Ahmed's chin still hurt – and it hurt a lot!

Then the doctor came in. He looked at Ahmed's chin. He wiped it with a special cloth and it burned a little. "Okay Ahmed," the doctor said. "Now you're going to have to be a brave boy. I'm going to stitch up your cut."

"What does that mean?" Ahmed asked, through tears.

"Well Ahmed, I need to sew it up. You see, your skin is ripped and so we have to sew it up, just like when your pants rip, and your mother sews up the rip."

"But I'm not pants! I'm a person! Please don't sew me up!" Ahmed said.

"Don't worry Ahmed," the doctor said. "You won't feel a thing. I'll give you a small needle to make you not feel the stitches. Now I need you to be very brave and hold very still."

Ahmed watched as the doctor took out his needle and a thread – he was really going to sew him up. Ahmed didn't want to be sewn up.

"I don't want to be sewn up," Ahmed said.

"It's the only way to stop the bleeding Ahmed," his father told him. His father held his hand tightly. "Say *Bismillah*."

Ahmed said *Bismillah*. The doctor started to stitch his chin – Ahmed saw the doctor put the needle in him and then take it out, and then in, and then out. He couldn't feel it, but he still didn't like it at all!

Ahmed held his father's hand tightly. In his mind, he said, *Bismillah, Bismillah, Bismillah*, over and over again.

"There, all done," said the doctor. "Now tell me Ahmed. How did you get that terrible cut?"

"I was just playing," Ahmed said.

"Oh, what kind of playing?" the doctor asked.

"Well I was jumping on the table, and – "

"Ahh, that explains it," said the doctor. "I get kids in here with bad cuts like yours, or even worse, and sometimes they even break their bones and it's all because they climb on the furniture or jump inside the house. Do you want to get a cut like this again, Ahmed?"

"No!" Ahmed said.

"Well then let me tell you what to do: You go to the park or go outside and there, you can jump all you want and you can climb, but not at home – a home is not for jumping and climbing. It's too dangerous, and you'll get hurt."

"Okay Doctor," said Ahmed.

"Okay, you take good care of yourself Ahmed," the doctor said, leaving the room.

"Thank you Doctor," Ahmed answered. "I will."

"*Alhamdulillah*. I'm glad you're safe," Ahmed's father said as he took him out to the car. He drove him home, where Mom, Dawud, and Haleema were waiting for him and they were all happy to see him and happy that his cut had finally stopped bleeding.

His mom took him up to his room and lay him down on his bed. "Oh my little Ahmed, I'm so happy to have you back safe and sound. Now you lie here and rest and I'll bring you some food."

His mother hugged him tightly.

"What happened at the hospital?" Dawud asked.

"Well, the doctor was really nice. He sewed up my cut. He said that some kids hurt themselves much worse than this," Ahmed told him.

"That's awful," said Dawud.

"But I sure learned my lesson," Ahmed said. "It's dangerous to jump and climb inside the house. I'll only do that at the park."

*****

SUGGESTED AGE GROUP
3 – 7 years old

BEHAVIORS ADDRESSED
• Dangerous behavior in the house, e.g., climbing furniture, jumping

BEHAVIORS MODELED
For Children
• To use Islamic phrases regularly, e.g.,*Assalaamu alaikum, Masha'a Allah, Jazaakum Allahu khairan*, etc.

• To say their different *duas* throughout the day

• To help their parents with house chores, e.g.,making their beds, setting the table, cleaning up their toys, etc.

• To share with their siblings

• For older siblings to help younger siblings learn to behave better, but not to be bossy

• To be gentle with their siblings

• To thank those who help them, e.g. the doctor

• Prophet Muhammad *saaw* said,
"Allah likes that whenever you do something, do the best that you can."
Reported by Aisha *raa*, narrated in Al-Baihaqei. E.g. when they cleaned up the table after breakfast.

For Parents

• Show affection and love to your children, but also discipline and train them

• Train your children for critical thinking by giving them choices and allowing them to make decision. E.g.when their mother has them choose their outfits for the day

• Encourage and compliment your children's abilities and don't focus only on their misbehaviors. E.g. when Ahmed's mother compliments his jumping, running, and climbing abilities at the park and on the way home.

• Fathers – show affection and interest in your children's activities. E.g. when their father asks how their day was when he comes home from work

• Support your spouse's authority in getting kids to do chores. E.g. when their father tells them to clean up and set the table before dinner, even though it's the mother that supervises.

• Train your children to help with house chores, but also train them and give them strategies of how to be careful when dealing with things that could break or spill, e.g. strategy of carrying out two plates at a time when Ahmed is setting the table

• Take your children outside to play so that they can expand their energy and exercise

CONCEPTS PRESENTED

• There are consequences for your actions, so if you make a bad choice, you will get bad results.

IMPORTANT NOTES

1. Does your child need to hear this story?

Children who do dangerous things that could result in them getting seriously hurt need to hear this story and to hear its drastic consequences. They need to be scared by these consequences to make them stop their dangerous behaviors so they don't get hurt.

If your children are not engaging in dangerous behaviors, they may not need to hear this story at all. I leave it to your discretion if your child needs to hear this story or not. I strongly recommend that you minimize the consequences and lessen how much Ahmed gets hurt, if your child is not acting dangerously and you choose to tell them this story. You do not want to scare your child needlessly.

2. A Must Do: When you are telling the story to your children, make sure to pause and comment about the character's bad behaviors while they are happening. Say things like "This is very wrong.", "How could they do such a thing?", "Oh, that's very bad." You can also ask the children if the characters are being "good or bad."

Although the story will show and explain this by the end, I strongly recommend that you don't wait until the end to present this. This way, your child will not associate the bad behaviors with being fun and glamorous.

The Clock

Once upon a time, there was a little boy named Mustafa. He was six years old and he lived with his mom, his dad, and his little sister Aya. He had many, many hobbies. Oh yes, Mustafa liked to do many things: he liked to play sports, he liked to draw, he liked to read, but Mustafa liked one thing most of all. What he liked the most was to party! Yes, he loved going over to his friends' houses and having parties with them. Sometimes Mustafa went to parties for the beginning of the school year and sometimes he went to parties for the beginning of summer, but of all the parties he had ever gone to, *Eid* parties were his favourite. He loved Eid parties because they were the most fun!

(Can ask the children if they like *Eid* parties here. Can ask them if they remember a fun *Eid* party.)

Now Mustafa was a very good boy, but there was one little thing that he did that his parents wished he wouldn't do – he played with their clock.

Mustafa would go into his parents' room and he would look at their clock with its red numbers. He thought it was really neat. He loved to see the numbers switch, but they switched so slowly, so he would speed them up. Mustafa would play with the buttons on his parents' clock and watch the clock count as quickly as it could, one number switching to the next and then the next. He would smile and laugh as he watched the clock count - he had a lot of fun doing this.

When his parents would come in and see Mustafa playing with the clock, they would shake their heads.

"Mustafa," they would say, "please don't play with the clock. Then we won't know what time it really is."

Well, Mustafa didn't want his parents not to know the real time, but he just had so much fun playing with the clock, that he did this again and again.

One day, only two days before *Eid*, Mustafa got some terrific news. Just as Mustafa was getting ready for bed, the phone rang.

RING! RING!

RING! RING!

"*Assalaamu alaikum*," his mother answered the phone.

Mustafa was changing into his pajamas in his room, but he could hear his mother talking from the living room. "Oh yes, how are you Zainab? . . . Yes, I'm doing well, *Alhamdulillah*. . . . Yes, . . . yes, . . . oh yes, I'm sure he would love that! Mustafa is here. Okay . . . . well he hasn't gone to bed yet. Sure, I'll get him for you."

Well Mustafa's mother didn't have to go very far to find him – he had heard her from his room, and he was very curious.

"What does Auntie Zainab want to tell me Mom?" he asked.

"Oh, well, I don't want to spoil the surprise, but it's actually Omar who wants to talk to you," his mother said. Omar was Auntie Zainab's son. He was one of Mustafa's best friends.

Mustafa held the phone to his ear. "*Assalaamu alaikum*," he said.

"*Wa'alaikum assalaam,* Mustafa," Omar answered. "I have a surprise for you."

"What is it?" Mustafa asked. Oooh boy, he loved surprises!

"Well . . ."

"Oh come on Omar, tell me! Tell me!"

"Okay, on Friday, the first day of *Eid*, I'm having something really special," Omar said.

"What? Are you watching a movie?" Mustafa asked.

"No," Omar said.

"Are you going to the park?" Mustafa asked.

"No," Omar said.

"Are you getting me a present?"

"Yeah, but that's not all. I'm having a party! And you're invited! Please say you can come! Please Mustafa, say you can come!" Omar pleaded.

"A PARTY?!" Mustafa cried. "Awesome! Oh Mom," he turned to his mother. "Please say I can go, Mom! Please say I can go!"

"Yes Mustafa," his mother said. "You can go to Omar's Eid Party."

"Oh YES! *Alhamdulillah!*" Mustafa celebrated. "I can come Omar! I can come!"

"Yay!" Omar cheered.

"Okay Mustafa, it's bedtime now," his mom said. "Say *Assaalamu alaikum* to Omar."

"Omar, I've got to go to bed," Mustafa said. "But I'll see you at the Eid Party!"

"Yeah! See you at my Eid Party! *Assalaamu alaikum* Mustafa," Omar said.

"*Wa' alaikum assalaam,*" Mustafa said and he hung up the phone. He turned to his mother with a big smile on his face. "I'm so excited for the party! Mom – this is the best! I love *Eid* parties! I can't wait for Friday! I can't wait for Omar's *Eid* Party! Love it! Love it! Love it!"

Mustafa was so excited – he was jumping up and down and up and down! This was terrific.

His mother smiled. "Yes, that is pretty exciting," she nodded. "But it's getting late, Mustafa. You'd better be off to bed."

Mustafa nodded and gave his mom a kiss and a hug goodnight. "*Assalaamu alaikum* Mom," he said.

"*Wa' alaikum assalaam* sweetie. Don't forget to brush your teeth."

Mustafa went into the bathroom and brushed his teeth. They were pearly clean. Then he headed out into the hallway and was walking to his room. As he passed his parents' room, he saw their clock, its bright red numbers were shining out at him. He stopped and looked in, then he took a step into his parents' room and a few more steps – one step, then another, then another – and there he was right in front of the clock. He reached out with his hands and pressed the buttons and he watched the clock count and count. But when he heard his father coming down the hallway, he turned around and headed out of the room.

"Mustafa," his father said, giving him a hug. "Good night. *Assalaamu aliakum*" and he walked him down to his room and tucked him into bed. All night long, Mustafa dreamt about the Eid party and how wonderful it would be.

The next day, early in the morning while Mustafa was still sleeping, there were some loud noises in the hallway. He woke up and wondered what was going on.

He sat up in bed and said his *dua*. *"Ashhadu an laa ilaaha illa Allah, wa ashhadu anna Muhammadan rasool Allah."*[24] Then he jumped out of bed and rushed out into the hall to see what was happening.

His mother and father were running around, from their room down to the kitchen.

"What's wrong?" Mustafa asked his father.

"I'm late. I'm late. I'm very, very late for work," his father said as he headed into the bathroom and closed the door.

"Hurry up," his mother called to his father from the kitchen. "I've packed you breakfast and lunch. You'll miss your meeting. Hurry Dear."

Mustafa headed into the kitchen to see his mother. *"Assalaamu alaikum* Mom," he said.

"Wa'alaikum assalaam Mustafa," she answered, but she didn't even look up at him. She was so busy running around, trying to get everything ready for his dad, that she didn't even give him his morning hug.

Then his father came in. He started rushing about the kitchen too.

"Mustafa, did you play with the clock again last night?" his father asked.

"Umm, yeah. I did."

"Mustafa, that's why I'm late. You can't play with it anymore. Do you understand?"

"Yeah. I'm sorry. I didn't mean for you to be late," Mustafa said. He felt bad. His father looked worried.

---

24. I bear witness that there is no God but Allah, and that Muhammad is the messenger of Allah.

"I just hope I catch this meeting at work," he said, grabbing his stuff and heading to the door. "It's very, very important. *Assalaamu alaikum.*"

"*Wa' alaikum assalaam,*" Mustafa and his mother answered.

"You really do need to stop playing with that clock you know," his mother said.

"I know," Mustafa said. "I'm sorry."

"Alright. Well go wash up for breakfast, Mustafa," she said.

And so Mustafa did. They had a big day ahead of them today. Tomorrow was *Eid* and they had many, many things to do. Today, Mustafa, Aya, and their mother were going to go out shopping. They were going to buy new *Eid* clothes for Aya and Mustafa. They were going to buy some cards to give to their friends at *Eid* prayer tomorrow. They were going to buy a present for Mustafa to take to Omar's big party tomorrow. That was a lot of shopping. So as soon as they had finished breakfast, they all got ready to go out for the day.

At the mall, Mustafa and Aya helped their mother choose some pretty cards for their friends. Then Aya found a beautiful dress that she wanted to wear for *Eid*. Then Mustafa looked and looked at all the different clothes. In the end he chose a pair of black pants and a green dress shirt and a funny tie. He tried them on and they looked very nice on him. He couldn't wait to wear them. Then it was time to choose Omar's present. Well, Mustafa looked and looked and looked. There were a lot of very nice toys, but he wanted to find the perfect present for Omar. First he looked at a package of Play-Dough – Omar liked Play-Dough. Then he saw a green ball. It was big and bouncy. Omar would like the ball, Mustafa thought. But then, he saw the perfect present for Omar. There it was on the shelf – a big, black, monster truck! Yeah, Omar loved trucks.

"I found it!" he announced to Aya and his mom. "I found the perfect present."

And so they bought the monster truck and headed out of the mall. All the way home in the car, all Mustafa talked about was the *Eid* party. He was so excited.

The whole rest of the day, all Mustafa talked about was the *Eid* party. He couldn't wait! He couldn't wait! He was so excited – he just couldn't wait!

"Oh, Mom," he asked her after lunch. "Can I please call Omar? I have some questions for him about the party."

"All right Mustafa, go ahead," she told him.

So he called Omar and they talked and talked. Mustafa wanted to know all about the party. He wanted to know what games they were playing, what food they were eating – he wanted to know everything. And he found out everything – it was going to be such an awesome party!

"Mom, Aya," he said when he got off the phone. "You'll never guess all the cool things that we're doing at the *Eid* Party tomorrow."

"What? What?" Aya asked.

"We're going to play Musical Chairs, Pin the Tail, Hot Potato, and Monopoly. And his Uncle has some surprise games for us too! It's so cool!"

"I wish I could go! You're so lucky!" Aya said.

"Yeah, it's going to be the best party ever!" Mustafa exclaimed.

"What time is the party?" Aya asked.

"It's from 5 to 7 exactly. Omar has to go to his Grandma's house after, so we can't be late at all. Okay Mom?"

"All right Mustafa," she agreed.

"Doesn't Omar have a sister who's having a party that I could go to?"

"No, he doesn't have any sisters," Mustafa said.

Aya frowned, "No fair. I wish my friends had cool *Eid* parties like yours."

"Oh Mom," Mustafa said. "I have an idea. Can I take brownies to the party tomorrow? The delicious super-duper yummy ones that you make? Can you make them for me? Please."

"You know Mustafa," his mother said. "I think it's wonderful that you want to take brownies and I have an idea for you. Why don't you make the brownies yourself? I'll show you how and then you can make them and I'll help you."

"Oh can I help too? Please?" Aya said.

"Sure!" exclaimed Mustafa. He was really excited. He had never made brownies before.

Mustafa got down to work. His mother showed him how and he let Aya help him, but these were his brownies. He measured the flour and the cocoa and the oil and the milk and all the other ingredients. He put them all in the big bowl and he stirred and he stirred. He took a lick – mmm mmm they were good!

He gave Aya a lick. "Yummy!" she said. Even his mother took a lick, "*Masha'a* Allah, you are a good baker," she said.

When the batter was all mixed up, his mother put the pan in the oven and left it to bake.

Mustafa and Aya went to play with their toys in his room, but all they talked about was the party. Mustafa couldn't wait. When the brownies were done, Mustafa's mom called him over to see them. He looked at them and they looked good! He smelled them and they smelled even better! He was so excited. He had baked his very own brownies – he couldn't wait to take them to the party tomorrow and share them with all his friends.

When his father came home from work, Mustafa showed him his new *Eid* clothes and he showed him the present that he had bought for Omar.

"Oh *Masha'a* Allah – Omar will like that," his father said.

And he showed him the brownies he baked for the party. His father was so proud of him.

Then they all sat down to eat dinner together. All through dinner, Mustafa talked about the *Eid* party. He talked about his friends and he talked about the games they would play and the brownies they would eat. Aya asked him one question after another after another and he answered them all.

After dinner, his father helped him wrap the *Eid* present for Omar and then he helped him cut the brownies into just the right number of pieces so that everybody at the party would eat one big piece.

"Oh I'm so excited for the party Dad," Mustafa said.

"Yeah, it seems like it's going to be great!" his father agreed.

When their parents took them to bed, Mustafa and Aya were both very excited. Tomorrow was *Eid*. They had their *Eid* clothes laid out and they couldn't wait for tomorrow's *Eid* prayers. Mustafa couldn't wait for the *Eid* party! Their Mom and Dad tucked them into bed and they said their prayers and fell off to sleep. All night long, Mustafa dreamt of the wonderful *Eid* party. He dreamt of how his friends would love his brownies, of how Omar would love the present he got him, of how he would play and play and play and party with his friends.

The next morning, Mustafa was so excited that he woke up very early. He went to his parents' room, but they were still asleep. He went into the kitchen and looked at his brownies – they looked so yummy. He couldn't wait for the party. He went back to his room and looked at his *Eid* clothes. He wished it were time to go to the party right now! He waited and he waited and he waited, until finally his parents woke up. They all ate breakfast and got dressed in their nice, new *Eid* clothes, and they headed off to *Eid* prayer. There, Mustafa saw his friends. "*Eid Mubarak*," he told them. They prayed all together and sat quietly during the *Eid Khutbah*[25]. Then, after the *Khutbah* was over, all of Mustafa's friends played with him and talked about the party. All of them couldn't wait to go!

After *Eid* prayer, Mustafa, Aya, and their parents went back home. Some of his parents' friends came to visit them for *Eid*. But all day long, all Mustafa thought about was the party. He wished it were time to go to the party now.

He went into his room and played with Aya for a while. He waited for five o'clock to come so he could go to the party. Then he went outside to his parents' and their visitors.

"Mom, Dad, is it time to go to the party yet?" he asked.

---

25. *Eid* prayer talk

"Not yet," they told him.

So he went back inside and played with Aya a little more. He thought about the party. "I wish it was party time," he told Aya and he waited and he waited. Then he went outside to his parents and their visitors.

"Dad, Mom, is it time to go to the party yet?" he asked.

"Not yet," they told him.

"Mustafa," his father said. "Can you please take this book inside and put it on my desk?"

"Sure thing, Dad." He took the book and went into his parents' room. He put it on his dad's desk and he turned to leave the room. He walked passed the dresser – there was the clock with its bright red numbers. He stopped in front of it and pressed the buttons – the clock started counting quickly, changing one number after the next. He stood there, watching the numbers switch.

"Mustafa," called Aya. "Come on. I need your help!"

Mustafa ran out of the room and went to see Aya.

"Can you draw a rabbit for me in my picture?" she asked.

"Okay," he agreed. He sat down and drew the picture for Aya. Mustafa sat and drew for a while, but all he could think about was the party. He wanted to go now. He waited and he waited. Then he went outside to his parents. Their visitors had left and they had gone to rest in their room.

"Mom, Dad, is it time to go to the party yet?" he asked.

"Not yet," they told him.

So he went back inside and he tried to read. He tried to play with his blocks, but he just wanted to go to the party. He got his present ready and he put it by the door. He was all ready – he just wished five o'clock would come!

He waited and he waited and he waited. Every little while he went to his parents' room and asked them if it was time to go to the party yet, but every little while, they said it still wasn't time and Mustafa had to wait some more.

Finally, it was time to go the party. He dressed up in his party clothes and he took his brownies and he took the present for Omar and he went out. The whole ride there, Mustafa was so excited.

Mustafa sang happily in the car:

"It's finally party time! It's finally party time!" he sang to his father. "I can't wait to see Omar and all my friends! I can't wait to play all these games! I can't wait for my friends to eat my brownies!"

Finally they pulled up to Omar's house. Mustafa ran out and rang the doorbell. He was so excited to see all his friends.

DING DONG

DING DONG

Mr. Reeyad opened the door.

"*Assalaamu Alaikum*," Mustafa said." We are here for the party."

"The party?" Mr. Reeyad said. "The party's over. It's seven thirty already!"

Mustafa's father looked at his watch, "You are right," he said. "My watch says seven thirty. Hmmm, but the clock at home said five. Mustafa did you play with my clock again?"

"Yes," Mustafa said sadly.

"We told you not to play with that," Mustafa's father said. "You see, because you played with the clock, we didn't know what time it really was and you missed the party."

"But I made the brownies for the party!" Mustafa said. "I brought a present for Omar! I want to see my friends! I want to play the games!" Mustafa said.

"I'm sorry – all your friends have already played and eaten and they've all gone home," Mr. Reeyad said.

"Well, can I at least see Omar?" Mustafa asked. By now there were tears in his eyes and a big lump in his throat. He felt so sad – he was going to cry.

"I'm really sorry Mustafa," Mr. Reeyad said. "But Omar has already gone to his Grandmother's house."

"Thank you Mr. Reeyad," his father said. Then he took Mustafa and went back to the car. On the ride home, Mustafa was very sad – he wished he had never played with the buttons on the clock. He had wanted to go to the party and see Omar and his other friends so much, but he had missed it. From that day on, Mustafa never played with the clock again.

*****

SUGGESTED AGE GROUP
3 – 8 years old

BEHAVIORS ADDRESSED
• Playing with their parents' clock
• See notes for how to customize this story & use it to correct other similar behaviors (e.g. playing with parent's keys, playing with light switches, playing with the switches for the heater, etc.)

BEHAVIORS MODELED

For Children

• To say the *Shahada* as soon as they wake up
• To say their prayers before going to sleep
• To help out their siblings and be nice to them
• To use Islamic phrases regularly, e.g. *Assalaamu alaikum, Masha'a* Allah, *Jazaakum Allahu khairan*, etc.

For Parents

• Kiss and hug your children at bedtime, in the morning, and throughout the day
• Deal with wrong behavior without yelling or venting anger at your children
• Make a big deal out of *Eid* – make children feel that it is really special
• Build your children's confidence through developing their skills. E.g. baking brownies for the party

• Give lots of encouragement in an exaggerated way that suits the child's exaggerated emotions. E.g.when his mother compliments Mustafa's baking

• Chat and talk as a family during dinner time, and listen to your children talk about what they are interested in and excited about

CONCEPTS PRESENTED

• There are consequences for your actions, so if you make a bad choice, you will get bad results

IMPORTANT NOTES

A Must Do: When you are telling the story to your children, make sure to pause and comment about the character's bad behaviors while they are happening. Say things like "This is very wrong.", "How could they do such a thing?", "Oh, that's very bad." You can also ask the children if the characters are being "good or bad."

Although the story will show and explain this by the end, I strongly recommend that you don't wait until the end to present this. This way, your child will not associate the bad behaviors with being fun and glamorous.

Arabic Terminology

Introduction

Most Islamic books contain Arabic terms that are frequently used throughout the books. These words seem to constitute a basic vocabulary that must be available to the reader. In the following glossary of Arabic terms, we attempt to provide most of the terms used in this book with their definitions.

GLOSSARY OF ARABIC TERMS

TERM	Definition
aa	Stands for *Alayhi Assalaam* "Peace be upon him"
Abee	Father in arabic
Alhamdulillah	All praise is due to Allah *SWT*
assalaamu alaikum wa rahmatullahi wa barakaatuh	The greeting of Muslims. It means Peace, mercy, and blessing of Allah be upon you
Asr	The third daily prayer, at mid-afternoon
Bismillah Ar-rahmaan Ar-rahim	In the name of God, most gracious most merciful
dua	Supplication
Eid	The Muslim celebration after the month of *Ramadan* and at the time of pilgrimage
Eid Mubarak	May you have a blessed *Eid*
Fajr	Dawn. Usually applies to the first obligatory prayer of the day, after dawn but before Sunrise

TERM	Definition
Hoyoo	Mother in Somalian
Insha'a Allah	God willing
Jannah	Paradise, Heaven
Jazaki Allahu khairan	May Allah reward you
Jazana wa iyakum	May He reward you too
Khutbah	Religious speech given by a knowledgeable person as part of either the Friday or the *Eid* sermon
Maghrib	The fourth daily prayer, at sunset
Masha'a Allah	Literally, "Whatever Allah wills." Usually used as an expression of admiration or glorification of Allah for something that is very pleasing or that has been done well
Qur'an	The word of Allah revealed to Prophet Muhammad *saaw* through Arc Angle Jebreel
raa	Stands for *radeya Allah anho* "May Allah be pleased with him/her"
saaw	May Allah's peace and blessings be with him
swt	Glory be to Him the Exalted
Seerah	The biography of the Prophet Muhammad *saaw*

TERM	**Definition**
Shahada	Linguistically speaking means witness. However, in religious context, it is used to indicate "There is no god except the one and only true God "Allah" and Muhammad is His messenger"
tarbiyah	The art of dealing with human nature by guiding people to make the right decisions and to improve by gently coaching and training to make sure that they are close to Allah, that they make the right decision and become better people
Thuhr	The second prayer of the day, around noon time
Wa'alaikum assalaam	And peace be upon you too

References

————.*The Noble Qur'an, English Translation of the Meanings and Commentary.* Medina, Kingdom of Saudi Arabia: King Fahd Complex for the Printing of the Holy Qur'an, 1417 A.H.

Beshir, Dr. Ekram and Mohamed Rida Beshir. *Meeting the Challenge of Parenting in the West, An Islamic Perspective,* 2nd ed. Beltsville, Maryland: Amana Publications, 2000.

Collins, Chase. *Tell Me A Story: Creating Bedtime Tales Your Children Will Dream On.* New York, New York: Houghton Mifflin Company, 1992.

Imam Abi Al-Husain Muslim Ibn Al-Haggag Al-Qushairee Al-Naisabouree. *Sahih Muslim,* 1st ed. Cairo, Egypt: Dar Ihiaa' Alkutob Alarabia, 1955.

Imam Abi Abdellah Muhammad Ibn Ismail Ibn Ibraheem Ibn Al-Mogheirah Ibn Bardezabah Al-Bukhari. *Sahih al-Bukhari.* Cairo, Egypt: Dar Al Shaa'b, n.d.

Khaled, Khaled Muhammad. *Khulafaa' Ar-Rasool (Successors of the Messenger,)* 2nd ed. Beirut, Lebanon: Dar Al Kitaab Al-'Arabee, 1974.

Khaled, Khaled Muhammad. *Rijaal Hawl Ar-Rasool (Men Around the Messenger).* Cairo, Egypt: Dar Al Kutub Al-Islaamiah, 1981.

Myers, David G. *Social Psychology,* 6th ed. Boston, Massachusetts: McGraw-Hill, 1999.

Qutb, Dr. Muhammad. *Manhaj At-Tarbiyah Al-Islaamiah (Program of Islamic Tarbiyah),* vol. 1. Cairo, Egypt: Dar Al Shuruq, 1981.